CHRISTMAS RECIPES

The Best Hot Cocoa Cookbook for the Holidays

(A Must-have Christmas Gift Cookbook for Everyone)

Phillip Salgado

Published by Alex Howard

© **Phillip Salgado**

All Rights Reserved

Christmas Recipes: The Best Hot Cocoa Cookbook for the Holidays (A Must-have Christmas Gift Cookbook for Everyone)

ISBN 978-1-989891-95-7

All rights reserved. No part of this guide may be reproduced in any form without permission in writing from the publisher except in the case of brief quotations embodied in critical articles or reviews.

Legal & Disclaimer

The information contained in this book is not designed to replace or take the place of any form of medicine or professional medical advice. The information in this book has been provided for educational and entertainment purposes only.

The information contained in this book has been compiled from sources deemed reliable, and it is accurate to the best of the Author's knowledge; however, the Author cannot guarantee its accuracy and validity and cannot be held liable for any errors or omissions. Changes are periodically made to this book. You must consult your doctor or get professional medical advice before using any of the suggested remedies, techniques, or information in this book.

Table of contents

Part 1 1

Exquisite Christmas Recipes 2

Chapter I - Desserts 3

Recipe 1: Switzerland - Brunsli (Chocolate Spiced Brownie Cookies) 3

Recipe 2: Australia - Fruity Pavlova 6

Recipe 3: Sweden - Julpepparkakor (Christmas Pepper Cookies) 8

Recipe 4: Chile - Pan de Pascua (Christmas Bread) 11

Recipe 5: Spain - Turron de Chocolate (Chocolate and Almond Christmas Candy) 15

Recipe 6: Colombia - Buñuelos Colombianos (Fried Cheese Balls) 17

Recipe 7: San Marino _ Bustrengo (Fig and Apple Cake with Honey) 19

Recipe 8: Denmark - Risalamande (Creamy Rice Pudding with Almonds) 21

Recipe 9: Philippines - Bibingka (Sticky Coconut Cake) 23

Recipe 10: Holland - Speculaas (Christmas Spiced Cookies) 25

Recipe 11: Malta - Pastizzotti tal-Qastan (Mini Chestnut Tarts) 28

Recipe 12: Hungary - Beigli (Hazelnut Filled Rolled Pastries) 30

Recipe 13: Jamaica - Black Rum Cake 33

Recipe 14: Italy - Parrozzo (Chocolate Covered Almond Cake) 36

Chapter II - Soups, Snacks, and Sides 38

Recipe 15: Norway - Savory Caraway Waffles 38

Recipe 16: England - Pigs in Blankets 41

Recipe 17: Albania - Byrek me Kungull dhe Arre (Pumpkin Pie) 43

Recipe 18: Wales - Cawl (Lamb and Root Vegetable Stew)...46

Recipe 19: Armenia - Itch (Bulgur Salad) 49

Recipe 20: Scotland -Traditional Cock a Leekie Soup 51

Recipe 21: China - Spiced Red Cabbage 53

Recipe 22: Russia - Dried Mushroom Soup 55

Recipe 23: Czech Republic - Vánocní Rybí Polévka (Christmas Fish Soup) 57

Recipe 24: New Zealand - Fresh Barbecued Crayfish 60

Recipe 25: Finland - Lanttulaatikko (Rutabaga casserole)....62

Recipe 26: Mexico - Ensalada De Nochebuena (Fruity Salad with Pomegranate Vinaigrette) 64

Recipe 27: Germany - Kartoffelpuffer (Bavarian Potato Pancakes) 66

Chapter III – Mains 68

Recipe 28: USA - Shrimp, Andouille and White Bean Cassoulet 68

Recipe 29: Brazil - Pork Tenderloin with Dried Apricots and Gouda Mascarpone Filling 72

Recipe 30: Iceland - Partridge with Blueberry Thyme Sauce 75

Recipe 31: Puerto Rico - Pernil Asado (Roast Pork Shoulder) 78

Recipe 32: Canada - Hot Smoked Sockeye Salmon with Charred Orange and Maple Syrup 80

Recipe 33: Poland - Christmas Carp with Wine 83

Recipe 34: Cyprus - Pork, Leek and Fennel Ragout (Hirino Me Prasa) 85

Recipe 35: Japan - Homemade Krispy Fried Chicken 88

Recipe 36: Ethiopia - Doro Wot (Chicken Stew) 91

Recipe 37: Ireland - Spiced Beef Rib 95

Recipe 38: France - Glazed Honey Roast Pork with Apples .. 97

Recipe 39: India - Mutton Biryani 99

Recipe 40: Greece - Veal Stew with Plums, Apricots, and Almonds 102

Part 2 104

Popular Christmas and New Year Recipes 105

1) Traditional Honey Glazed Ham 106

2) Bacon Wrapped Dates 108

3) Charleston Style Breakfast Casserole 110

4) Tasty Pork and Sauerkraut 112

5) Chocolate Dipped Strawberries 114

6) Easy Roasted Veggies 116

7) Delicious Sweet Potato Casserole 118

8) Hearty Black-Eyed Pea Gumbo 120

9) Healthy Kale and Yam Salad 122

10) Christmas Style Pear Salad 125

11) Homemade Tamales 127

12) Delicious Eggnog 130

13) Cheese and Ham Party Sandwiches 132

14) Decadent Banana Bread 134

15) Appetizer Cocktail Meatballs 136

16) Easy Spinach Dip 138

17) Tasty Prime Rib 140

18) Easy Baked Kale Chips 142

19) Decadent Chocolate Trifle 144

20) Apple Caramel Pork Chops 146

21) Cheesy Baked Tortellini 149

22) Filling Cheese and Broccoli Soup 151

23) Easy Squash Risotto 153

24) Tasty and Decadent Carrot Cake 156

25) Classic Artichoke Bruschetta 159

26) Creamy Lentil Soup 161

Part 1

Exquisite Christmas Recipes

Chapter I - Desserts

Recipe 1: Switzerland - Brunsli (Chocolate Spiced Brownie Cookies)

These spiced chocolate cookies smell almost as divine as they taste. With a flavor similar to gingerbread, and a texture halfway between a brownie and a cookie, these sweet little bites are a scrumptious blend of all our favorite holiday treats.

Yield: 40-60*

Preparation Time: 10mins

Cook Time: 5mins

Total Cook Time: 8hours 15mins

Ingredient List:

- 1 pinch sea salt
- 5 ounces granulated sugar
- 9 ounces ground almonds
- Pinch ground cloves
- ¼ teaspoons ground cinnamon
- 2 tablespoons plain flour
- 2 tablespoons cocoa powder
- 2 egg whites
- 3½ ounces bittersweet chocolate (chopped small)
- Boiling water
- 2 teaspoons kirsch cherry liqueur
- Equipment:
- Festive cookie cutters

Instructions:

1. Line a cookie sheet with parchment paper. Set aside.

2. Sift together the salt, sugar, almonds, cloves, cinnamon, flour and cocoa powder into a mixing bowl.

3. Whisk in the egg whites until incorporated.

4. Add the chopped chocolate to a bowl, cover with just enough boiling water to melt the chocolate. Do not stir, allow to stand for 5 minutes, carefully pour away all but ½ a tablespoon of the water. Stir well until silky smooth and pour into the dough mixture along with the kirsch. Knead until combined.

5. Roll the dough out into a ⅓-½" sheet. Use the cookie cutters to cut out different shapes, and place them on the prepared cookie sheet.

6. Set aside in a dry place overnight.

7. Preheat the main oven to 300 degrees F.

8. Bake the cookies in the oven for approximately 5 minutes, allow to completely cool before enjoying.

*Depending on the size of the cookie cutters.

Recipe 2: Australia - Fruity Pavlova

An Australian Christmas celebration would be incomplete without a show-stopping Pavlova; layers of crunchy chewy meringue, slathered with sweet cream and bursting with fresh juicy fruit.

Yield: 2-4

Preparation Time: 15mins

Cook Time: 1hour

Total Cook Time: 2hours 15mins

Ingredient List:
- 4 egg whites
- 1 cup + 5teaspoons caster sugar
- 1 teaspoon white vinegar
- 1 tablespoon cornflour
- 2⅛ cup whipping cream

- ½ cup granulated sugar
- 1½ teaspoons vanilla essence
- Fresh fruit (for topping)

Instructions:

1. Preheat the main oven to 375 degrees F, line a baking sheet with parchment paper.

2. Whip the egg whites with the sugar, using an electric mixer, for 10 minutes, until glossy and thick.

3. Beat in the white vinegar and cornflour for another 5-6 minutes.

4. Spoon the meringue mixture onto the baking sheet in a 7-8" circle. Smoothing the surface.

5. Place in the oven and turn the temperature to 220 degrees F. Bake for 60 minutes.

6. When baked, turn the oven off and crack open the oven door. Allow the Pavlova to cool completely in the oven before removing.

7. Transfer the meringue to a serving plate.

8. In a bowl, whip together the cream, sugar and vanilla essence, until fluffy and cloud-like, spoon the mixture onto the meringue and top with fresh fruits.

9. Serve!

Recipe 3: Sweden - Julpepparkakor (Christmas Pepper Cookies)

Julpepparkakor translates to Christmas pepper cookie, thanks to its spicy gingerbread flavor. This flavorsome dough is cut into pretty shapes and decorated with white icing; they are even used as decorations in some homes.

Yield: 36

Preparation Time: 15mins

Cook Time: 3hours 30mins

Total Cook Time: 3hour 45mins (plus 3 days standing time)

Ingredient List:
- 1 cup white sugar
- 1 cup salted butter (room temperature)
- 1 egg

- ½ cup molasses
- 3¼ cups all-purpose flour
- 1 tablespoon cinnamon
- 1 tablespoon powdered ginger
- 2 teaspoons cloves
- 1 teaspoon bicarb of soda
- Flour (for work surface)
- Butter (for greasing)
- White icing (to decorate)

Instructions:

1. Cream together the sugar and butter. Beat in the egg and molasses.

2. In a separate bowl, combine the flour cinnamon, ginger, cloves and bicarb of soda.

3. Add the flour mixture to the butter mixture, a little at a time, until incorporated.

4. Split the dough into two equal pieces. Form each piece into a disc and cover with plastic wrap. Chill for 1-2 hours.

5. Preheat the main oven to 350 degrees F and grease two cookie sheets.

6. Lightly flour your work surface. Roll out each piece of chilled dough to a ¼" thick sheet.

7. Use festive cookie cutters to cut shapes out of the dough and arrange them on the cookie sheets.

8. Place in the oven and bake for 8-10 minutes.

9. Allow to cool completely on wire baking racks before decorating with icing.

Recipe 4: Chile - Pan de Pascua (Christmas Bread)

Chile's answer to panettone, pan de Pascua, is a sweet yeast bread rich with dried fruit. The recipe is believed to have travelled to Chile in the 1900s with German immigrants who also favor a bread-like cake during Christmas time.

Yield: 8

Preparation Time: 15mins

Cook Time: 55mins

Total Cook Time: 3hour 50mins

Ingredient List:

Sponge:

- ½ cup warm water (105-115 degrees F)
- Pinch white sugar
- 1 (0.25 ounce) envelope of active dry yeast

- ¾ cup all-purpose unbleached flour

Dough:
- ½ cup unsalted butter (softened)
- ⅓ cup granulated sugar
- ½ teaspoons sea salt
- Zest of 1 orange (finely grated)
- 4 eggs (at room temperature)
- 3 cups all-purpose flour (unbleached)
- 1½ teaspoons vanilla essence
- 1½ teaspoons brandy
- ½ cup glace cherries
- ⅔ cup raisins (mixed dark and golden)
- ⅓ cup candied lemon peel
- 1 tablespoon unsalted butter (melted)

Instructions:

1. First, make the sponge. In a glass jug (2 cup capacity), add the water and pinch of sugar. Sprinkle with the dry yeast, stir and allow to stand for 5-6 minutes, until foamy.

2. Add the flour and cover with a piece of plastic wrap. Set aside for approximately 25 minutes, at room temperature. Remove the plastic and stir to deflate the mixture a little. Set to one side.

3. Now prepare the dough; using an electric mixer to beat together the butter and granulated sugar for 5-6 minutes.

4. Add the salt and orange zest, beat until combined.

5. With the mixer running, crack in the eggs one at a time, scraping down the bowl as necessary. Pour in the yeast mixture and stir until incorporated.

6. Turn the mixture to a low speed and add 2 cups of the flour, when combined add the remaining cup of flour along with the vanilla essence and brandy, beating until smooth.

7. Turn the speed up to medium for 5-6 minutes, beating the dough until it's texture becomes elastic.

8. Fold in the cherries, raisins and candied lemon peel until well incorporated.

9. Grease a large sized bowl with melted butter. Set to one side for a moment.

10. Tip the dough out onto your work surface, using cleans hands, roll it into a ball. Place the ball in the greased bowl and gently roll it to coat in the butter.

11. Cover the bowl with plastic, kitchen wrap. Set aside for an hour in a draft-free, warm place until the dough doubles in size.

12. Take a 3" high, 9" wide, springform tin and grease.

13. Turn the dough out of the bowl and knead for 60 seconds before placing in the greased tin. Cover again with plastic wrap and once again set aside for an hour in a draft-free, warm place, until the dough doubles in size.

14. Preheat the main oven to 375 degrees F and place the rack in the bottom third of the oven.

15. Take the plastic wrap off the dough and place in the oven, bake for 20-25 minutes before removing and loosely fitting a sheet of aluminum foil on top of the loaf. Bake for another half an hour.

16. Take the cake out of the oven and cool in the tin for 15 minutes before turning out. Allow to cool completely before slicing and serving.

Recipe 5: Spain - Turron de Chocolate (Chocolate and Almond Christmas Candy)

Turron is undoubtedly the most loved and popular Christmas candy. This chewy nougat-like sweet treat is of Moorish origin. It was first made over 500 years ago in the small town of Jijona, where wildflowers grew plentifully, bringing an abundance of honey; turron's staple ingredient.

Yield: 6

Preparation Time: 10mins

Cook Time: 2mins

Total Cook Time: 7hours 12mins

Ingredient List:

- 8 ounces semisweet chocolate (broken)

- 8 ounces 60% cocoa dark chocolate (broken)
- 1 tablespoon water
- 2½ ounces vegetable shortening (at room temperature)
- 3 ounces roughly chopped almonds
- 2¾ ounces puff rice cereal

Instructions:

1. Add the broken chocolates along with the water to a medium bowl and melt in the microwave for approximately 90-120 seconds, removing at 20 second intervals to stir.

2. Immediately add the shortening and stir well until it is incorporated.

3. Stir in the almonds and puff rice cereal until well distributed.

4. Spoon the mixture into 5x7" container (preferably silicone, but plastic will work too).

5. Tightly cover with plastic wrap and refrigerate for 6-7 hours.

6. Use a knife to run around the edges of the container to loosen the turron and turn out onto a chopping board.

7. Cut the turron into ¼" slices.

Recipe 6: Colombia - Buñuelos Colombianos (Fried Cheese Balls)

In Colombia, the holidays are a very social time where families celebrate the Novena de Aguinaldos (the days leading up to Christmas). They visit friends, family and neighbors to eat, drink, pray and sing carols. These little bunuelos will definitely be on the menu, served alongside hot cocoa or strong coffee.

Yield: 8-12*

Preparation Time: 10mins

Cook Time: 10mins

Total Cook Time: 20mins

Ingredient List:
- ¾ cup cornstarch
- ¼ cup tapioca starch

- 1 cup queso casteno (finely grated)**
- ½ cup queso fresco (finely grated)***
- 2 medium eggs
- ¼ teaspoons baking powder
- 2 tablespoons granulated sugar
- Pinch sea salt
- 1 tablespoon whole milk
- Vegetable oil (for deep frying)

Instructions:

1. Add the cornstarch tapioca stark, queso casteno, queso fresco, eggs, baking powder, sugar, sea salt and milk into a mixing bowl and combine using clean hands.

2. Roll the dough into small-medium, smooth balls.

3. Pour the vegetable oil into a deep pot and bring to a temperature of 300 degrees F.

4. Drop the balls in the oil and cover. Fry for approximately 3 minutes, before turning the heat up to brown the balls until golden.

5. Remove from the oil using a slotted spoon and rest on kitchen paper towel for a few seconds before serving.

*Depending on the size of the balls.

**If you cannot source queso casteno, feta cheese is a suitable alternative.

***If you cannot source queso fresco, fresh farmer's cheese is a suitable alternative.

Recipe 7: San Marino _ Bustrengo (Fig and Apple Cake with Honey)

Traditionally this delicious little cake is cooked in a copper pot over hot coals on a fireplace, don't worry it tastes just as delicious when baked in the oven.

Yield: 8-10

Preparation Time: 5mins

Cook Time: 55mins

Total Cook Time: 1hour

Ingredient List:
- Butter (for greasing)
- 2 cups plain flour
- ½ cup cornmeal
- 1½ cups stale breadcrumbs
- 3 medium eggs
- ¼ cup olive oil

- ½ teaspoons sea salt
- 5 tablespoons organic honey
- 2 cups whole milk
- 1 pound sweet apples (cored, peeled, diced)
- 3 ounces chopped dried figs
- 3 ounces raisins
- Zest of 1 medium lemon (finely grated)
- Zest of 1 medium orange (finely grated)

Instructions:

1. Preheat the main oven to 325 degrees F. Lightly butter a baking dish (9x13").

2. In a bowl, combine the flour, cornmeal, breadcrumbs, eggs, olive oil, and salt.

3. Whisk in the honey and milk.

4. Add the apples, figs, raisins, lemon zest and orange zest and stir gently until combined.

5. Pour the batter into the prepared dish and place in the oven. Bake for approximately 55 minutes.

6. Serve warm.

Recipe 8: Denmark - Risalamande (Creamy Rice Pudding with Almonds)

Rice pudding is the most traditional way to round off the Christmas feast. Thick, warming and creamy; it's the perfect winter dessert. To prepare it like a true Dane; before serving, place a whole almond in one of the serving bowls, whoever finds it will have good luck for the New Year.

Yield: 6

Preparation Time: 10mins

Cook Time: 30mins

Total Cook Time: 45mins

Ingredient List:

- 7 ounces uncooked pudding rice
- 3⅓ cup whole milk

- 1¾ ounces caster sugar
- Scrapings of 1 vanilla pod
- 2⅔ ounce whole almonds
- 1¼ cups double cream

Instructions:

1. In a heavy-bottomed saucepan, add the rice, milk, sugar and vanilla pod scrapings. Stir well.

2. Cook over moderate heat for approximately half an hour, stirring occasionally until all of the milk has been absorbed.

3. Take off the heat and allow to cool for 10-15 minutes.

4. Set one almond aside and chop the rest finely.

5. Fold the chopped almonds into the rice pudding until incorporated.

6. In a separate bowl, whip up the cream until fluffy and fold it gently into the rice pudding

7. Spoon the pudding into bowls. Press the single, whole almond down into the pudding in one of the bowls and switch the bowls around until you no longer know which bowl contains the lucky nut.

8. Serve!

Recipe 9: Philippines - Bibingka (Sticky Coconut Cake)

Bibingka is a moist and dense cake adored by kids and grownups! Bursting with tropical flavor, thanks to the coconut cream and crushed pineapple, it's easy to see why.

Yield: 18-20

Preparation Time: 10mins

Cook Time: 60mins

Total Cook Time: 1hour 30mins

Ingredient List:
- Butter (for greasing)
- 2 cups white sugar
- 8 ounces full-fat cream cheese
- 3 medium eggs
- 1 pound sweet rice flour
- 1 tablespoon baking powder

- ½ cup salted butter (melted)
- 1 tablespoon vanilla essence
- 1 (15 ounce) can cream of coconut
- 1 cup whole milk
- 8 ounces canned crushed pineapple
- ¼ cup light brown sugar
- 2 tablespoons white sugar

Instructions:

1. Preheat the main oven to 350 degrees F. Grease a 9x13" pan.

2. In a bowl, beat together the sugar and cream cheese.

3. Beat in the eggs, one at a time, until incorporated.

4. Add the flour, baking powder, melted butter, vanilla essence, cream of coconut, milk, and pineapple. Stir well until totally combined.

5. Pour the batter into the prepared tin. Sprinkle with the light brown and white sugar.

6. Place in the oven and bake for 60 minutes. Allow to completely cool before slicing into squares and serving.

Recipe 10: Holland - Speculaas (Christmas Spiced Cookies)

These crunchy, caramelized biscuits have a deliciously buttery spiced flavor. They're traditionally baked for St. Nicholas' Day on the December 5th and are often decorated with impressive designs, depicting classic Christmas stories.

Yield: 30

Preparation Time: 15mins

Cook Time: 10mins

Total Cook Time: 5hour 20mins

Ingredient List:
- 1 cup salted butter (room temperature)
- 1 cup brown sugar
- 2 medium eggs
- 2 teaspoons orange peel (grated)

- 1 tablespoon molasses
- 3½ cups all-purpose flour
- 1 teaspoon baking powder
- ½ cup almonds (finely ground)
- 3 teaspoons cinnamon
- ½ teaspoons cloves
- ½ teaspoons nutmeg
- ¼ teaspoons white pepper
- ¼ teaspoons ginger powder
- ¼ teaspoons cardamom
- Milk and slivered almonds (for decorating)

Equipment:

- Festive-shaped cookie cutters (floured)

Instructions:

1. Cream together the butter and brown sugar in a large bowl.

2. Beat in the eggs, orange peel and molasses.

3. In a separate bowl, combine the flour, baking powder, almonds, cinnamon, cloves, nutmeg, white pepper, ginger powder, and cardamom.

4. Add the flour mixture to the egg mixture. a little at a time, mixing well between each addition. Cover the dough and chill for 4-5 hours.

5. Preheat the main oven to 350 degrees F and line a cookies sheet with parchment paper.

6. Cover your work surface with a piece of parchment paper, turn the dough out onto the paper and roll into an even ⅛" disc.

7. Flour your cookie cutters and cut shapes out of the dough. Re-roll and re-use the pastry scraps.

8. Place the biscuits on the cookie sheet. Brush each biscuit with a little milk and sprinkle with almonds.

9. Place in the oven and bake for approximately 8-10 minutes.

10. Allow to cool on wire baking racks before serving.

Recipe 11: Malta - Pastizzotti tal-Qastan (Mini Chestnut Tarts)

Maltese people are known to have a super sweet tooth, so it comes as no surprise that they help to celebrate Christmas with these sweet little chestnut tarts. These mini morsels were traditionally served alongside a strong cup of coffee and a glass of orange flower water.

Yield: 40-50*

Preparation Time: 15mins

Cook Time: 35mins

Total Cook Time: 10hours 50mins (plus 3 days standing time)

Ingredient List:
- 14 ounces dried chestnuts
- 1¾ tablespoons hot chocolate powder

- ½ cup sultanas
- 3½ ounces white sugar
- Pinch ground cloves
- Pinch ground cinnamon
- Zest of 1 medium orange
- Zest of 1 medium lemon
- 1⅔ pound sweet pastry dough

Instructions:

1. Add the chestnuts to a bowl and cover with water. Set aside for 10 hours.

2. In a saucepan add the soaked chestnuts along with additional water, bring to a simmer and cook until the nuts are soft.

3. Pass the mixture through a fine-mesh sieve to drain away the water.

4. Add the nut mixture to a bowl along with the hot chocolate powder, sultanas, white sugar, cloves, cinnamon, and zests. Mix until well combined.

5. Roll out the dough and press into your tart tin. Be sure to leave enough leftover pastry to cut into strips and arrange in a lattice pattern on top of each tart.

6. Spoon the chestnut mixture into the pastry cases.

7. Place in the oven and bake for approximately 25 minutes.

8. Allow to cool to warm before serving, or enjoy cold.

*Depending on the size of the tart tin.

Recipe 12: Hungary - Beigli (Hazelnut Filled Rolled Pastries)

Originating in Germany in the 19th century, this recipe sees sweet dough spread with a yummy hazelnut paste. The pastries are rolled before being baked and sliced into moreish pin-wheel pastries.

Yield: 10-12

Preparation Time: 15mins

Cook Time: 35mins

Total Cook Time: 1hour 15mins

Ingredient List:

Filling:

- ½ cup walnuts (very finely chopped)
- 1 cup granulated sugar
- ¼ cup whipping cream
- Pinch ground cinnamon

- ¼ cup raisins
- 2-3 drops vanilla essence
- 1 tablespoon organic apricot jam
- 2 teaspoons lemon peel (grated)

Pastries:

- Butter (for greasing)
- Flour (for surface)
- 8 ounces refrigerated dough
- 2 tablespoons water
- 1 egg yolk
- 1 tablespoon confectioner's sugar

Instructions:

1. In a small saucepan, add the walnuts, sugar, and cream. Heat until thickened.

2. Add the cinnamon, raisins, vanilla, jam and lemon peel, stir well and heat until totally combined.

3. Transfer to a bowl, cover with plastic wrap and allow to cool completely.

4. Preheat the main oven to 350 degrees F. Grease a baking sheet and set aside.

5. Lightly flour your work surface and roll out the dough.

6. Spread the cooled filling in an even layer over the dough, leaving a ½" border. Roll the dough into a log, using the long side.

7. Place on the baking sheet, seam-side down.

8. Whisk together the water and egg yolk. Brush the mixture over the pastry roll.

9. Set aside at room temperature for 10-12 minutes.

10. Place in the oven and bake for 15 minutes before removing and lightly covering with a piece of foil. Bake for a final 5-10 minutes.

11. Allow to completely cool on a wire rack before slicing.

Recipe 13: Jamaica - Black Rum Cake

For many Jamaicans, the sight of grandmother in the kitchen whipping up a batch of black rum cake is their favorite holiday memory. Similar to British plum cake but with a punchier edge, thanks to the rum, Jamaican Christmas cake is a must try!

Yield: 10-12

Preparation Time: 15mins

Cook Time: 3hours 30mins

Total Cook Time: 3hour 45mins (plus 3 days standing time)

Ingredient List:
- 8 ounces golden raisins
- 8 ounces dried pitted prunes
- 4 ounces mixed fruit peel
- 8 ounces currants
- 8 ounces maraschino cherries

- 2 cups port
- ½ cup rum (preferably Jamaican)
- ½ pound brown sugar
- ½ pound salted butter
- 1 teaspoon baking powder
- ½ pound plain flour
- ½ teaspoons nutmeg
- 1 teaspoon cinnamon
- Pinch sea salt
- 6 eggs
- ½ teaspoons almond essence
- 1 teaspoon vanilla essence
- Few drops browning sauce
- ½ cup rum (preferable Jamaican, for brushing)

Instructions:

1. In a re-sealable glass jar add the raisins, prunes, fruit peel, currants, and cherries. Pour over the port and rum. Seal the jar and set in a cool, dark place for 3 days.

2. Preheat the main oven to 300 degrees F and line a 9" baking tin with parchment paper.

3. Cream together the brown sugar and salted butter until fluffy.

4. In a separate bowl sift together the baking powder, flour, nutmeg, cinnamon, and salt.

5. Beat the eggs into the butter/sugar mixture, one egg at a time, until combined.

6. Fold the dry flour mix into the wet mix in batches.

7. Add the dried fruit mixture along with the almond and vanilla essence. Mix well.

8. Add a few drops of browning sauce if the batter is too pale (it should be a rich dark brown).

9. Pour the batter into the tin and place in the oven for approximately 1½ hours; turn the oven down to 250 degrees F and bake for another 2 hours, until the cake is set in the center.

10. To preserve the cake, when cool, brush with the rum and then wrap with a layer of wax paper, followed by a layer of aluminum foil. Store in a dry, cool place.

Recipe 14: Italy - Parrozzo (Chocolate Covered Almond Cake)

Celebrate the holidays Italian style with a slice of this Abruzzese dome cake covered with a crunchy, bitter almond, dark chocolate shell.

Yield: 10

Preparation Time: 10mins

Cook Time: 1hour 5mins

Total Cook Time: 1hour 30mins

Ingredient List:
- Butter and flour (for greasing)
- 6 medium eggs (separated)
- 7 ounces granulated sugar
- Zest of 1 medium lemon (grated)
- 5⅓ ounces ground almonds
- 5⅓ ounces semolina

- 1½ tablespoons bitter almond essence
- 7 ounces dark chocolate (chopped)

Instructions:

1. Preheat the main oven to 325 degrees F. Grease and flour a dome-shaped cake mold.

2. In a bowl, whip the egg whites with the granulated sugar until foamy. Add the egg yolks and mix with a wooden spoon.

3. Add the lemon zest and almonds, whisk the mixture until smooth and then add the semolina. Whisk again until combined.

4. Pour batter into the prepared mold and place in the oven. Bake for approximately 60 minutes.

5. Set the cake aside to cool.

6. In the meantime, using a double boiler, melt together the almond essence and chopped chocolate. Stir together until glossy. Pour the melted chocolate over the cooled cake. Allow to completely set before slicing.

Chapter II - Soups, Snacks, and Sides

Recipe 15: Norway - Savory Caraway Waffles

Norwegians are very traditional when it comes to Christmas fare, and most families continue to enjoy Norwegian Christmas food throughout the holiday season. These caraway waffles served with lumpfish or salmon roe make an excellent appetizer and pair exceptionally well with chilled Champagne.

Yield: 8-10

Preparation Time: 20mins

Cook Time: 7mins

Total Cook Time: 30mins

Ingredient List:

- 1¼ cups flour

- ½ teaspoons salt
- ½ teaspoons baking powder
- 2 teaspoons whole caraway seeds
- 1 cup mashed potatoes
- 1¼ cups buttermilk
- 2 medium eggs (beaten)
- 2 tablespoons butter (melted, cooled)
- 1 cup sour cream
- Salmon roe or lumpfish
- Gravlax (optional)
- Capers (optional)

Instructions:

1. In a mixing bowl, combine the flour along with the salt, baking powder and caraway and whisk until combined.

2. In a second medium bowl, add the mashed potatoes to the buttermilk, and beaten eggs along with the cool melted butter and using a whisk, mix to break up any large lumps. The batter will, however, remain a little lumpy. Allow the batter to rest for 10 minutes.

3. In the meantime, while the batter rests, preheat a lightly greased waffle iron.

4. When you are ready to begin cooking, check that the batter is not too thick, if it is too thick, gradually add additional buttermilk; up to 2 tablespoons of buttermilk should be sufficient.

5. Once the batter is your desired consistency, pour ¾ cup of batter into the waffle iron.

6. Cook for approximately 3-5 minutes, or until the waffles are browned. Remove the waffles from the waffle iron, snipping apart with kitchen scissors, and serve at once with sour cream and salmon roe or lumpfish.

7. Alternatively, top with gravlax and capers.

Recipe 16: England - Pigs in Blankets

Turkey with all the trimmings just isn't the same without these tasty bacon-wrapped sausages. They make great party nibbles.

Yield: 16

Preparation Time: 15mins

Cook Time: 15mins

Total Cook Time: 30mins

Ingredient List:

- 8 slices streaky bacon (thinly sliced)
- 16 chipolata sausages

Instructions:

1. Preheat the main oven to 400 degrees F.

2. Arrange the bacon on a cutting board, and using the sharp edge of a kitchen knife, stretch and flatten the slices of bacon until they are approximately half as long again; this will help to make the bacon crispier.

3. Slice each piece of bacon in half across, and wrap around a sausage, rolling until the sausage is encased.

4. Secure with a toothpick.

5. Place in a roasting pan and roast for 12-15 minutes or until a little gnarly looking, golden brown and sufficiently cooked through.

Recipe 17: Albania - Byrek me Kungull dhe Arre (Pumpkin Pie)

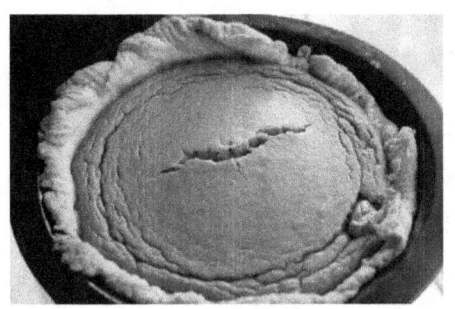

A traditional pumpkin and walnut pie, cooked on Christmas Eve. Served as either a sweet and nutty side dish, a snack or even as dessert. This festive pie is a firm Albanian favorite.

Yield: 12

Preparation Time: 15mins

Cook Time: 1hour 30mins

Total Cook Time: 2hours 45mins

Ingredient List:

- 1⅛ cup salted butter
- 1 pound butternut squash (peeled, seeded, chopped)
- 1¼ cups whole milk (divided)
- 3 medium eggs

- 1 tablespoon flour
- ½ teaspoons salt
- Olive oil (to grease)
- 12 sheets filo pastry
- 2-3 cup walnuts (chopped)
- 1 cup water

Instructions:

1. First, prepare the filling. Melt the butter in a saucepan and add the chopped butternut squash and gently simmer for 25-30 minutes, or until the pumpkin is softened.

2. Turn the heat off and over a jug, sieve the pumpkin's juices. Put the juice aside.

3. In a food blender, puree the softened pumpkin.

4. In a large mixing bowl, combine ¾ cup of milk, with the 3 eggs, flour and ½ teaspoon of salt. Add a little over ¾ cup of pumpkin juice and stir to combine. Stir in the pureed pumpkin and mix well to prepare the filling; the consistency should be more of a liquid rather than a mash.

5. Next, make the pie by greasing a large, circular 12" baking dish with olive oil; ideally, the dish needs to be at least 3" deep.

6. Layer half of the pastry sheets, on top of one another in the dish, allowing the pastry to overhang the dish.

7. Dribble the remaining milk onto each of the pastry layers and using clean hands, gently rub it into the sheets of pastry.

8. Scatter the top of the puree with chopped nuts, making sure they are evenly spread.

9. Finally, layer the remaining 6 sheets of pastry over the top of the walnuts, using the same method as before.

10. Roll the overhanging pastry to make a crust around the circumference of the pumpkin pie.

11. Pour the remaining ½ cup of milk over the top of the pie and use a pastry brush to distribute it evenly.

12. Place the pie in the lower third of the oven and bake for 35-40 minutes at 375 degrees F, until crispy and golden.

13. Take out of the oven and immediately pour the water over the top and around the edges. Cover the pie with a clean tea towel or cloth and set aside to cool for 60 minutes before slicing and serving*.

*It is usual for the underneath to be a little soft and soggy.

Recipe 18: Wales - Cawl (Lamb and Root Vegetable Stew)

Every Christmas a number of the castles in Wales hold Medieval Nights. Here, guests take part in regal banquets, listen to period music and enjoy a feast fit for a king. Welsh Cawl, which is a hearty lamb and root vegetable soup, is always at the top of the menu.

Yield: 8

Preparation Time: 35mins

Cook Time: 1hour 30mins

Total Cook Time: 10hours 5mins

Ingredient List:

- 2 teaspoons sea salt
- 1 large onion (peeled)
- 2 pounds 2 ounces bone-in, lamb neck fillet (cut into 2" chunks)

- 2 pounds 2 ounces swede (peeled, diced)
- 2 medium carrots (peeled, diced)
- 2 Maris Piper potatoes (peeled, cut into even quarters)
- 2 parsnips (peeled)
- 3 large leeks (stripped, outer leaves discarded, cut into ½" slices)
- Pepper
- Caerphilly cheese (to serve)
- Crusty bread (to serve)

Instructions:

1. Add 2 quarts of water, and 2 teaspoons of sea salt to a large stock pot, over high heat, bring to the boil.

2. Add the whole peeled onion to the pot along with the lamb. Return to boil, and using a metal spoon skim off any surface foam.

3. Simmer for 10-15 minutes, or until cooked through.

4. Using a slotted kitchen utensil, remove the lamb from the pot and put to one side to cool.

5. Strip the lamb meat from the bone and return the meat to the pot.

6. Add the diced swede to the pot and bring to the boil until tender, 10-15 minutes.

7. Add the carrots to the pot, bring to boil, and simmer for 15-20 minutes, covered, until just tender.

8. Next, add the potatoes to the pan, bring to boil, and simmer, covered, until tender, 15-20 minutes.

9. Add the parsnips and the majority of the leeks to the pot. Bring to boil, then to simmer for 10 minutes, covered, until tender.

10. Taste and season accordingly, add the uncooked leeks (held back in the previous step).

11. Cover the pot and when cooled, transfer to the refrigerator to chill, overnight.

12. As soon as you are ready to serve, simmer gently until the cawl is sufficiently warm.

13. Ladle the cawl into soup bowls, season with pepper, and serve alongside a large wedge of Caerphilly cheese and crust bread.

Recipe 19: Armenia - Itch (Bulgur Salad)

This fresh grain salad is often served during Christmas and the New Year as either a snack or side dish with dinner. It's a little like tabbouleh.

Yield: 8

Preparation Time: 5mins

Cook Time: 20mins

Total Cook Time: 35mins

Ingredient List:
- ½ cup olive oil
- 1 large onion (peeled, finely diced)
- 1 large green bell pepper (finely diced)
- 4 garlic cloves (minced)
- 2 cups chopped tomatoes
- 1 teaspoon salt

- ½ teaspoons ground cayenne pepper
- 1 cup water
- 2 cups fine bulgur
- Juice of 1 large lemon
- 5 medium green onions (sliced)
- ½ cup fresh parsley (chopped)
- Extra virgin olive oil (to drizzle)

Instructions:

1. In a large frying pan or skillet over moderate heat, warm the olive oil. Add the onion along with the green pepper and cook for 7-8 minutes, or until the onion begins to soften.

2. Add the garlic and cook for 60 seconds.

3. Stir in the tomatoes, and add the salt, and cayenne pepper, cover and cook for 10 minutes.

4. Add the water along with the fine bulgar, stirring to coat.

5. Cover the pan with a lid and on low heat cook for another 10 minutes.

6. Remove the pan from the heat, stir well to combine, cover and allow to rest for 10 minutes.

7. Cool to room temperature and stir in the freshly squeezed lemon juice. Transfer to the refrigerator.

8. When you are ready to serve top with green onions, parsley, and drizzle with oil.

Recipe 20: Scotland -Traditional Cock a Leekie Soup

This soup goes back all the way back to the 16th century and is a traditionally served on Burns Night. It is also an ideal soup to serve the day after Christmas.

Yield: 6

Preparation Time: 1hour 30mins

Cook Time: 30mins

Total Cook Time: 2hours

Ingredient List:
- 2 pounds 12ounces fresh, whole free range chicken
- 12 medium leeks (washed, chopped to 1" lengths, divided)
- 4 ounces long grain rice (washed)
- 4 medium carrots (peeled, grated)
- 6 prunes

- Salt and black pepper

Instructions:

1. Place the chicken along with half of the leeks in a large pan or stockpot and add sufficient cold water to cover.

2. Cover the pot with a lid, and gently simmer for 60 minutes, or until the chicken meat falls easily off the bone).

3. Remove the pot from the heat and place the chicken on a large serving platter and cover with a clean tea towel to cool. Once completely cooled, it can be transferred to the fridge.

4. Strain the chicken broth into a large pan and add the rice. Cover with a lid and cook for 10 minutes, after which, add the grated carrots along with the remaining leeks and prunes. Continue to cook; uncovered, for a further 20 minutes.

5. Taste the broth and if necessary, reduce the liquid further until you are happy with the flavor and season well with salt and black pepper, to taste.

6. Chop a small amount of the reserved cooked chicken* into bite-sized pieces, transfer to soup bowls and ladle over the chicken broth and veggies to serve the traditional soup.

*The remaining chicken can be served in a pie, a casserole or any other suitable leftover recipe.

Recipe 21: China - Spiced Red Cabbage

There are very few Christians throughout China, and so the holiday is only celebrated in the big cities. It is only here that there are decorations and Christmas tree lights. For those people who do enjoy a Christmas meal, spiced red cabbage is a popular side dish.

Yield: 4

Preparation Time: 20mins

Cook Time: 2hours 5mins

Total Cook Time: 2hours 25mins

Ingredient List:
- 2 tablespoons olive oil
- 1 red cabbage (finely shredded)
- 3 tablespoons brown sugar
- 4 tablespoons balsamic vinegar
- 1 cinnamon stick
- 1 star anise

- 2 cloves
- 2 cooking apples (peeled, cored, chopped)
- Juice and peel of 1 medium orange

Instructions:

1. Over high heat, heat a large saucepan or pot.

2. Add the olive oil, followed by the shredded red cabbage and cook for 5 minutes. Stir in the brown sugar along with the balsamic vinegar.

3. Add the cinnamon stick, star anise, cloves, together with the apples, orange juice, and orange peel. Stir well to combine and cook over low heat for 2 hours, while occasionally stirring.

4. Taste and season accordingly.

Recipe 22: Russia - Dried Mushroom Soup

Hunting for mushrooms and drying them in preparation for Winter is a national pastime in Slavic countries. This Christmas recipe for mushroom soup is often served at the Russian Christmas Eve Holy Summer or 'sochevnik'.

Yield: 6 cups

Preparation Time: 30mins

Cook Time: 2hours 30mins

Total Cook Time: 3hours

Ingredient List:

- 2 cups dried mushrooms (broken into pieces)
- 8 cups cold water
- 1 teaspoon sea salt (to taste)
- 1 garlic clove
- 2 tablespoons onion (peeled, chopped)
- 1 tablespoon oil

Instructions:

1. Rinse the mushrooms under cold running water to remove any dirt.

2. In a saucepan, cover the mushrooms with the cold water, sea salt, and garlic.

3. Cover the pan and simmer for 2-2 ½ hours, or until the mushrooms are tender. Taste and season with salt as needed.

4. In a frying pan or skillet, sauté the onion in oil, until soft and add to the mushroom soup.

5. Simmer for 3-4 minutes.

Recipe 23: Czech Republic - Vánocní Rybí Polévka (Christmas Fish Soup)

This food soup is traditionally served to the needy in Prague's Old Town Square on Christmas Day at 6pm each year. This specialty soup is also the first course on Christmas Day for families throughout the Czech Republic. So why not add a Czechoslovakian recipe to your holiday menu?

Yield: 4-6

Preparation Time: 20mins

Cook Time: 1hour 5mins

Total Cook Time: 1hour 25mins

Ingredient List:
- 2-3 fillets of carp
- 1 pound carp (head and tail piece only)
- Salt

- 8 cups water
- 1 onion (peeled, sliced)
- 2 parsnips (peeled, finely chopped)
- 1 turnip (peeled, finely chopped)
- 2 carrots (peeled, finely chopped)
- 1 medium onion (finely chopped)
- 1 fish roe
- 4 tablespoons butter (divided)
- 2 tablespoons flour
- Dash nutmeg
- Salt and black pepper
- Chopped parsley (to garnish)
- Buttered croutons (to garnish)

Instructions:

1. First, cook the carp; the fillets, the head and the tail in a pan, filled with salted water, add the sliced onions and cook until the onion is softened; 20 minutes.

2. In the meantime, gently fry the parsnips, turnip, carrots, finely chopped onion, and fish roe in 2 tablespoons of butter until softened.

3. As soon as the stock is ready, add it to the veggies and put the fish to one side.

4. In a second pan, melt the remaining butter and add the flour, stirring until browned.

5. Pour in the soup and bring to boil, reduce the heat to a simmer for 30 minutes.

6. Add the fish set aside earlier, and add the nutmeg, seasoning well to taste.

7. When you are ready to serve, ladle the soup into bowls and top with parsley and buttered croutons.

Recipe 24: New Zealand - Fresh Barbecued Crayfish

New Zealand, being in the Southern hemisphere means that Christmas is celebrated in the middle of summer! And although lots of families do sit down to a traditional turkey or ham dinner with all the trimmings, BBQs and picnics are equally popular.

Yield: 8

Preparation Time: 10mins

Cook Time: 10mins

Total Cook Time: 20mins

Ingredient List:

- 4 fresh and live, medium crayfish
- Salt
- Drizzle of olive oil (to fry)
- ½ cup mixed fresh herbs (mint, parsley, basil)

- 4 tablespoons garlic butter
- Splash of lemon juice
- 8 slices wholemeal sliced bread
- 4 leaves iceberg lettuce
- 2 cups steamed long grain rice
- 3 sprigs mint (to garnish)
- 2 lemon wedges (to serve)

Instructions:

1. In a very large pot cover the crayfish with water for 30 minutes.

2. Bring a stockpot of salted water to a boil, add the crayfish and cook on a simmer for 4-6 minutes. Take the crayfish out of the water and put to one side to chill.

3. As soon as the crayfish is sufficiently cool, split in half lengthways.

4. Lightly grease or oil a hotplate, sprinkle with salt, then turn the heat on

5. Arrange the crayfish, meat siding facing down and grill for between 2-3 minutes on moderate heat. Turn the crayfish over and grill for 2 minutes. Generously sprinkle with herbs, garlic butter and a splash of lemon juice

6. Arrange the slices of wholemeal bread along with the lettuce leaves and steamed rice. Top with the crayfish, garnish with mint and wedges of lemon.

Recipe 25: Finland - Lanttulaatikko (Rutabaga casserole)

A traditional must-have casserole dish for Christmas. This dish is surprisingly satisfying and sweet and can be enjoyed either alongside a few other casseroles on the Christmas table and generally as a side dish to fish, ham, or other meats.

Yield: 6

Preparation Time: 10mins

Cook Time: 1hour 5mins

Total Cook Time: 1hour 15mins

Ingredient List:

- 2 (6 cups) medium rutabagas (peeled, diced)
- Water
- 3 tablespoons butter (divided, extra for greasing)
- ¾ cup half and half

- ¾ cup gluten-free breadcrumbs
- 1 teaspoon salt
- ½ teaspoons nutmeg
- 2 medium eggs (lightly beaten)

Instructions:

1. In a large saucepan, add the diced rutabaga and pour in sufficient water to cover. Bring to boil, reduce heat to simmer, and cook for 20 minutes, or until tender. Drain the rutabaga and mash. Set to one side to cool.

2. Preheat the main oven to 350 degrees F. Lightly grease an ovenproof casserole dish with butter.

3. Add 2 tablespoons of butter along with the half and half, breadcrumbs, salt, nutmeg and the lightly beaten eggs to the rutabaga and stir well to combine.

4. Pour the mixture into the casserole dish, dotting the top of the casserole with any remaining butter.

5. Bake in the oven for 40-45 minutes, or until the top is golden brown.

Recipe 26: Mexico - Ensalada De Nochebuena (Fruity Salad with Pomegranate Vinaigrette)

This colorful Mexican salad is served at Christmas Eve dinner. The combination of bright ingredients make this healthy dish especially festive.

Yield: 4

Preparation Time: 10mins

Cook Time: N/A

Total Cook Time: 10mins

Ingredient List:

Vinaigrette:

- ¼ cup extra virgin olive oil
- 3 tablespoons pomegranate juice
- 2 tablespoons freshly squeezed lime juice

- 2 teaspoons sugar
- ⅛ teaspoons cayenne pepper
- Kosher salt
- Black pepper
- 1 tablespoon fresh cilantro (chopped)

Salad:
- 1 (6 ounce) bag mixed greens
- 1 ¼ cups beets (cooked, sliced)
- 2 ruby red grapefruits (peeled, segmented)
- 1 Pink Lady apple (cored, diced)
- 1 cup jicama/Mexican turnip (julienned)
- ½ cup pomegranate arils

Instructions:

1. In a small mixing bowl whisk the oil along with the pomegranate juice, lime juice, sugar, cayenne pepper, salt, pepper, and cilantro.

2. In a large mixing bowl, combine the mixed greens, sliced beets, grapefruit segments, diced apple, julienned turnip and pomegranate arils, using wooden salad spoons, mix to combine.

3. Scatter the chopped cilantro over the vinaigrette, and pour over the salad, tossing well to combine.

Recipe 27: Germany - Kartoffelpuffer (Bavarian Potato Pancakes)

Savory golden pancakes are delicious served with applesauce and are the perfect snack. Alternatively, serve with egg and bacon for the perfect Christmas breakfast.

Yield: 8

Preparation Time: 10mins

Cook Time: 10mins

Total Cook Time: 20mins

Ingredient List:

- 2½ pounds russet potatoes (peeled, finely grated)
- 2 medium yellow onions (peeled, finely grated)
- ⅓ cup flour
- 3 medium eggs
- Kosher salt (to taste)

- Ground white pepper (to taste)
- Canola oil (for frying)
- Applesauce (optional, to serve)

Instructions:

1. Place the grated potatoes along with the onions in a strainer set over a mixing bowl and allow to drain, gently squeezing the vegetables until dry, before placing in a second bowl.

2. Gradually pour off the potato and onion water, until you are only left with milky starch. Pour this over the drained potato and onion mixture.

3. Add the flour together with the eggs and season well with kosher salt and white pepper; mixing well until incorporated.

4. In fry pan or skillet over moderate heat, heat ¼ cup of canola oil. Working in batches, take ½ cup of potato mixture, and using clean hands, flatten out to make a pancake (4-5"), add the pancakes to the frying pan and flipping over once, cook until golden and cooked through, between 6-8 minutes.

5. Transfer the pancakes to a kitchen paper towel lined plated.

6. Repeat the process until all of the mixture has been used.

Chapter III – Mains

Recipe 28: USA - Shrimp, Andouille and White Bean Cassoulet

In the 19th century in New Orleans, Reveillon; a meal eaten in the small hours of the morning, following the return of Creoles from Christmas Eve and New Years Eve's Midnight Mass became an ongoing tradition. Although guests were invited to the New Year's Eve feast, the Christmas Reveillon was a family event with grandparents taking places of honor. Only the best foods were chosen for the meal, and this shrimp and white bean cassoulet is just one of them.

Yield: 8

Preparation Time: 35mins

Cook Time: 2hours

Total Cook Time: 2hours 35mins

Ingredient List:

- 1 pound navy pea beans (soaked overnight)
- 5 bay leaves (divided)
- Creole seasoning (divided, to taste)
- 3 tablespoons olive oil
- 1 pound Andouille sausage (chopped into ¼ " pieces)
- 1 yellow onion (peeled, diced)
- 4 sticks celery (diced)
- 4 cloves garlic (minced)
- 1 teaspoon dried oregano
- 28 ounces canned whole peeled Roma tomatoes
- 3 teaspoons Worcestershire sauce
- 2 teaspoons fresh thyme
- 1 bunch scallions (chopped)
- 3 cups chicken stock
- 3 cups Panko breadcrumbs
- 1 ½ cups Parmesan (freshly shredded)
- 3 tablespoons olive oil
- Sea salt and black pepper
- 4 pounds medium Gulf shrimp (peeled, deveined)
- French bread (warm)

Instructions:

1. In a large saucepan or stock pot, add the soaked navy pea beans, along with 3 bay leaves, and the Creole seasoning. Cover the pea beans with sufficient water. Bring the water to boil; adding more water as needed, for 60 minutes, or until the beans are softened. Drain the mixture and put to one side.

2. In a Dutch oven, over moderate to high heat, heat the olive oil. Add the sausage and cook for 8-10 minutes, or until just browned.

3. Add the diced onion together with the celery, garlic, and oregano. Taste, and add additional Creole seasoning as needed, cook for 7-9 minutes, or until the veggies are just tender.

4. Using clean hands, crush the tomatoes, over the Dutch oven, and add to the pot.

5. Add 2 bay leaves, together with the Worcestershire sauce, the navy pea beans put to one side earlier, thyme and green onions. Pour in the chicken stock, and bring to boil.

6. Reduce the heat to moderate to low, and simmer for 15-20 minutes, or until the beans have absorbed the broth.

7. In the meantime, set the broiler on low.

8. In a mixing bowl, combine the breadcrumbs, with the Parmesan cheese, olive oil, sea salt, and black pepper. Put to one side.

9. Add the Gulf shrimp to the Dutch oven and cook for 8-10 minutes, or until the shrimp are pink.

10. Add the Panko mixture to the Dutch oven and place under the broiler, cooking for 2-3 minutes, or until the Panko is golden.

Recipe 29: Brazil - Pork Tenderloin with Dried Apricots and Gouda Mascarpone Filling

Brazilians celebrate Christmas on the evening of December 24 and food is served after midnight, on December 25. This recipe is a classic Brazilian Christmas supper; moist pork, with a sweet and creamy filling.

Yield: 6

Preparation Time: 15mins

Cook Time: 40mins

Total Cook Time: 36hours 55mins

Ingredient List:

Pork tenderloin:

- 1 (1¾ pounds) pork tenderloin

- Salt and black pepper
- 4 cloves garlic (minced)
- ½ cup aged balsamic vinegar
- ½ cup extra-virgin olive oil
- ½ cup scallions (chopped)
- ¼ cup rosemary leaves
- 1½ cups dried apricots (finely sliced)
- 5 ounces Gouda cheese (freshly shredded)
- ½ cup mascarpone
- ½ cup dry white wine

Instructions:

1. For the pork tenderloin: Butterfly the pork tenderloin by slicing it lengthwise, cut to the other side but avoiding cutting it right through. Open the halves and lay the tenderloin flat. Place the tenderloin between 2 pieces of plastic wrap. Using a rolling pin or meat mallet, pound the pork tenderloin to around a ½" thickness.

2. Transfer the pork tenderloin to a large chopping board and season well on each side with salt and black pepper. Set to one side.

3. In a medium-sized mixing bowl, combine the garlic along with balsamic vinegar, olive oil, scallions, and rosemary until incorporated.

4. Transfer the marinade along with the pork to a ziplock bag. Remove as much air from the bag as is

possible. Place the bag in the fridge for between 12 and 36 hours.

5. Preheat the main oven 400 degrees F.

6. In a medium-sized mixing bowl, combine the dried apricots with the shredded Gouda and mascarpone, mix well until combine. Set to one side.

7. Remove the pork tenderloin from the ziplock bag and lay flat on a clean working surface.

8. Add the dry white wine to the marinade and transfer to the fridge to keep cool.

9. Evenly distribute the apricot-cheese mixture over the pork. Roll the pork up and using cocktail sticks, at 1" intervals, secure.

10. Transfer the rolled up tenderloin to a baking dish and cover with foil. Bake in the oven for 25 minutes before removing the aluminum foil and covering with the marinade.

11. Return to the oven, uncovered for another 15 minutes, basting with the meat juices every 5 minutes during the cooking process.

12. Remove the pork from the oven and loosely cover with aluminum foil.

13. Allow to rest, while covered, for 8 minutes.

14. Remove the foil and place on large chopping board.

15. Drizzle the meat with the meat juices and serve.

Recipe 30: Iceland - Partridge with Blueberry Thyme Sauce

You've heard of the 12 Days of Christmas with a 'partridge in a pear tree,' now make this delicious Icelandic dish, which sees moist and juicy game served with a simply divine blueberry thyme sauce.

Yield: 4

Preparation Time: 15mins

Cook Time: 1hour 30mins

Total Cook Time: 1hour 45mins

Ingredient List:

- 4 (8 ounce) partridges (breasts removed, carcasses chopped)
- 2 tablespoons oil
- 1 medium carrot (chopped)

- 8 cups chicken broth
- 3 cups blueberries (half dried, half fresh)
- 2 bay leaves
- 1¼ teaspoons dried thyme
- 3¼ cups heavy cream
- 4 tablespoons chilled unsalted butter (cubed)
- Sea salt and black pepper

Instructions:

1. Heat the oil in a large, deep saucepan. Add the partridge carcasses and cook over moderate-high heat for 6-7 minutes.

2. Add the carrot and cook for 5-6 more minutes. Pour in the broth along with the blueberries, bay leaves, and thyme. Bring to a boil, then reduce to a simmer for 60 minutes, skimming any fat from the surface.

3. Strain the sauce into a clean saucepan and return to the heat for 20 minutes, until reduced to 1 cup.

4. In a medium saucepan, simmer the heavy cream until it's reduced to half its original volume. Pour the cream into the strained stock and whisk.

5. Take off the heat and whisk in 2 tablespoons butter, sea salt, and black pepper. Keep the sauce warm while you prepare the partridge.

6. In a 12" skillet, melt the remaining butter over a moderately high heat.

7. Sprinkle the partridge breasts with sea salt and black pepper. Place in the pan and cook for 4-5 minutes each side.

8. Slice the cooked partridge and serve with the sauce.

Recipe 31: Puerto Rico - Pernil Asado (Roast Pork Shoulder)

This pork shoulder is the epitome of Puerto Rican party food. In actual fact, Pernil is a holiday meal centerpiece, and ideal for any big family celebration or get together.

Yield: 8

Preparation Time: 15mins

Cook Time: 5hours

Total Cook Time: 11hours 15mins

Ingredient List:

- 1 cup freshly squeezed orange juice
- 1/2 cup red wine vinegar
- 1/3 cup light brown sugar
- 1/4 cup sea salt
- 1/4 cup black pepper

- 2 tablespoons virgin olive oil
- 2 tablespoons each dried oregano, ground cumin
- 35 garlic cloves (minced)
- 1 (8 pound) skin-on, bone-in, pork shoulder

Instructions:

1. In a mixing bowl, combine the orange juice along with the wine vinegar, light brown sugar, sea salt, black pepper, olive oil, dried oregano, cumin, and garlic, set the marinade to one side.

2. Place the pork in a roasting pan.

3. Using a kitchen paring knife, cut 1" deep, 1 ½ "wide slits all over the pork shoulder.

4. Pour the marinade over the pork shoulder and transfer to the fridge to chill for a minimum of 5-6 hours.

5. Place in an oven set at 325 degrees F, and roast the pork, basting with the marinade every 25 minutes, or until a thermometer inserted into the very thickest part of the meat registers, 190 degrees, this will take around 4-5 hours. Allow to rest before serving.

Recipe 32: Canada - Hot Smoked Sockeye Salmon with Charred Orange and Maple Syrup

When Canadians sit down to Christmas dinner this year, chances are the star of the show will be the turkey. However, you can be sure for non-meat eaters salmon will feature very heavily on the menu.

Yield: 6

Preparation Time: 2hours

Cook Time: 45mins

Total Cook Time: 2hours 45mins

Ingredient List:

- 2 medium oranges
- 2 cups brown sugar
- 1 cup kosher salt

- 1 tablespoon black pepper
- 1 teaspoon ground juniper berries
- 1 teaspoon ground coriander seed
- 2 (½ pound) salmon fillets
- 1 cup maple syrup

Instructions:

1. Using a fine grater box, zest both of the oranges and put to one side, ready for grilling later on.

2. Next, make the salmon cure by combining the brown sugar along with the kosher salt, black pepper, juniper berries, and coriander seeds. Mix well to combine.

3. Take the salmon fillets and coat on both sides with the salt and spice mix.

4. Lay the salmon fillets, skin side facing down on a baking sheet, lined with parchment paper. Allow to rest in the refrigerator for 1 ½ hours.

5. Rinse the salt and spice mix off the salmon fillets using cold running water, and pat dry with kitchen paper towel.

6. Set up your smoker.

7. Place the salmon fillets into the smoker.

8. Make sure that the smokers' internal temperature is between 120-140 degrees F, with full smoke.

9. Brush the salmon fillets with maple syrup and place in the smoker, return to the smoker every 4 to 5 minutes and brush with additional syrup.

10. The fillets will need to smoke until they flake easily when using a fork, around 4-5 minutes.

11. Using a sharp knife, slice the oranges in half, and place cut side facing up, under the broiler, and allow to roast until they are nicely charred.

12. When you are ready to serve, squeeze the orange juice from the charred fruit on top of the salmon fillets.

Recipe 33: Poland - Christmas Carp with Wine

You won't find meat on a Polish dinner table on Christmas Eve. What you will find though, is carp served in a red wine, honey, nut and raisin sauce.

Yield: 4-6

Preparation Time: 15mins

Cook Time: 1hour 30mins

Total Cook Time: 1hour 45mins

Ingredient List:
- 3 tablespoons unsalted butter
- 3 tablespoons + extra all-purpose flour
- 2 cups fish stock
- 1 cup dry red wine
- ¼ cup slivered almonds
- 2 tablespoons organic honey

- 4 tablespoons raisins
- Sea salt and black pepper
- 1 teaspoon powdered ginger
- Juice of ½ medium lemon
- 1 (3-4 pound) carp (scaled, gutted)
- 3 tablespoons canola oil
- Fresh parsley (for garnish)
- Lemon wedges (for garnish)

Instructions:

1. In a saucepan, melt the butter over medium heat.

2. Add the 3tbsp flour and whisk until smooth, cook for 2-3 minutes.

3. Pour in the stock and wine, whisk well and the sprinkle in the almonds, honey, and raisins.

4. Simmer over a low heat for 15 minutes, stirring occasionally.

5. Season with sea salt and black pepper.

6. Add the ginger and lemon juice. Keep the sauce warm while you prepare the fish.

7. Cut the fresh carp into steaks and season with sea salt and black pepper. Dip each steak in flour to lightly coat.

8. In a sauté pan, heat the oil until nearly smoking. Add the fish and cook for 5-6 minutes each side, until golden.

9. Serve the fish immediately with the sauce.

10. Garnish with fresh parsley and lemon wedges.

Recipe 34: Cyprus - Pork, Leek and Fennel Ragout (Hirino Me Prasa)

After observing 40 days of fasting, Cypriots can look forward to the Christmas feast. Pork and lamb feature heavily on the holiday menu, and this simple ragout is full of festive flavor.

Yield: 8

Preparation Time: 30mins

Cook Time: 1hour 30mins

Total Cook Time: 2hours

Ingredient List:

- 1⅓ cups of olive oil
- 4½ pounds pork shoulder (cut into 3" chunks)
- 1 pound of ripe tomatoes (quartered)
- 1 bunch wild celery or (chopped)

- 1 bunch fresh fennel (chopped)
- 2 ½ pounds of fresh leeks (cleaned, sliced into 4-5" pieces, halved lengthwise)
- 2 ¼ pounds of potatoes (peeled, cut into half)
- ⅔ cup lightly concentrated tomato juice
- 1 tablespoon salt
- Juice 1 lemon

Instructions:

1. In your pressure cooker over moderate heat, heat the oil.

2. Add the pork and stir to evenly coat with the olive oil and without sealing, cover.

3. Allow to gently brown, occasionally stirring, for between 7-10 minutes.

4. Add 2 ¾ cups of water and bring to boil, cover and seal. As soon as pressure has been reached, lower the heat and continue cooking for 20 minutes. Remove from the heat and using fast release, pressure down.

5. Place the tomatoes, in the bowl of a blender, and using a multifunctional blade, process on setting number 2 for 6-7 seconds.

6. As soon as it is safe to do so, open the pressure cooker, and add the celery, chopped fennel, and fresh leeks, packing the mixture down, and return to a moderate heat.

7. Bring to boil, and continue cooking for 10 minutes, occasionally stirring; as the leeks soften and reduce in

actual size (this is important as the pressure cooker must not be too full when in the lock position).

8. Add the tomatoes, while stirring, along with the tomato juice, 1 tablespoon of salt and bring to boil. Close and seal.

9. As soon as pressure is achieved, reduce the temperature, and cook for 15 minutes. Remove from the heat, and pressure down, with fast release, while carefully opening the pot.

10. Add the potatoes, return to moderate heat, stirring well, and bring to boil. Cover and seal. As soon as pressure is achieved, reduce the heat, and continue cooking for 5 minutes.

11. Remove from the heat and using fast release, pressure down.

12. Open the cooker, add the freshly squeezed lemon juice and stir to combine.

13. Put the top on the pot, without sealing, and allow to sit for 20-25 minutes before dishing up.

Recipe 35: Japan - Homemade Krispy Fried Chicken

While the rest of us dream of turkey and all the trimming, in Japan a fried chicken fast- food is the star on the top of the tree! Over 3 ½ million families eat takeout fried chicken, with literally millions of Japanese families forming long lines to order their Christmas chicken weeks before Christmas.

Yield: 4

Preparation Time: 20mins

Cook Time: 40mins

Total Cook Time: 1hour

Ingredient List:

Spice mix:

- 1 tablespoon paprika

- 2 teaspoons onion salt
- 1 teaspoon chili powder
- 1 teaspoon black pepper
- ½ teaspoons celery salt
- ½ teaspoons dried sage
- ½ teaspoons garlic powder
- ½ teaspoons allspice
- ½ teaspoons oregano
- ½ teaspoons basil
- ½ teaspoons marjoram
- Fried chicken;
- 1½ cups all-purpose flour
- 1 tablespoon brown sugar
- 1 tablespoon kosher salt
- 2 chicken breast, 2 thighs, 2 drumsticks, 2 wings
- 1 medium egg white
- 2 quarts cooking oil (for frying)

Instructions:

1. Preheat a deep fat fryer to 350 degrees F.

2. In a small mixing bowl combine all 11 of the spice mix ingredients, in recipe order (paprika, onion salt, chili powder, black pepper, celery salt, dried sage, garlic powder, allspice, oregano, basil and marjoram).

3. Combine the 11 ingredient spice mix with the flour, brown sugar and salt.

4. Dip each piece of chicken in egg white and evenly coat. Next, dip the chicken pieces in the flour-salt

mixture. Flip the chicken over 2-3 times to ensure that the flour mix adheres to the chicken.

5. Repeat until all the chicken is coated.

6. Put the chicken to one side for 4-5 minutes, for it to dry.

7. In batches, fry the coated chicken pieces. The breast and wings will take between 12-15 minutes, and the thighs and legs should take 3minutes more.

8. The chicken is cooked through when a meat thermometer, when inserted into the thickest part of the chicken, registers 165 degrees F.

9. Allow the chicken to drain on few sheets of kitchen paper towel to absorb any excess fat.

10. Serve the fried chicken hot.

Recipe 36: Ethiopia - Doro Wot (Chicken Stew)

This hot and spicy meal is in fact, Ethiopia's National dish. Christmas in Ethiopia falls on January 7th rather than December 25th and this slow cooked, comforting dish is perfect for all the family.

Yield: 6

Preparation Time: 45mins

Cook Time: 1hour 20mins

Total Cook Time: 2hours 5mins

Ingredient List:

Spiced butter:

- 1 pound unsalted butter
- 1 small onion (coarsely chopped)
- 3 tablespoons garlic (finely chopped)
- 1-2 tablespoons ginger root (finely chopped)
- 1 teaspoon ground cumin

- 1 teaspoon cardamom
- 1 teaspoon dried oregano
- ½ teaspoons ground turmeric
- ¼ teaspoons grated nutmeg
- 5-6 Basil leaves
- 1 teaspoon fenugreek seeds

Berbere Spice:

- 3 tablespoons smoked paprika
- 2 tablespoons paprika
- 1 tablespoon ground ginger spice
- 1 tablespoon granulated garlic spice
- 1 tablespoon dried basil
- 1 teaspoon freshly ground white pepper
- ½ tablespoons cinnamon spice
- ½ tablespoons ground nutmeg spice
- ½ tablespoons fenugreek
- 1 teaspoon cumin
- 1 teaspoon cardamom spice
- 1 tablespoon hot pepper chili,
- Cayenne pepper (to taste)

Chicken:

- 1 (3½ pound) whole chicken (cut into pieces)
- Salt and pepper
- 3 tablespoons spiced butter
- Canola oil
- 3 medium onions sliced
- 2 tablespoons berbere Spice
- 1 tablespoon minced garlic

- ½ tablespoons minced ginger
- Water
- 1 tablespoon tomato paste
- 1 tablespoon dried basil optional
- 6 large soft-boiled eggs (peeled)

Instructions:

1. To prepare the spiced butter: In a saucepan over low heat, melt the butter. Simmer without allowing the butter to brown, and until the butter foams.

2. Skim all of the foam off, while cooking until the mixture looks transparent.

3. Next, add the onion, garlic, ginger, cumin, cardamom, oregano, turmeric, nutmeg, basil and fenugreek, cook over low heat for 15-20 minutes.

4. Pass the butter through a sieve or piece of clean cheesecloth.

5. Store in a re-sealable container in the fridge until you are ready to use.

6. To make the Berbere spice: In a pan, cook all of the spices until they are toasty and emit a fragrance. Remove from the pan and using a coffee grinder, grind.

7. Transfer to a bowl, stir well to combine.

8. Store in a re-sealable container until ready to use.

9. Next, make the Doro Wot.

10. Season the chicken with salt and pepper and put to one side.

11. Heat a large pot, over moderate heat, until hot. Add the spiced butter along with a little oil and the onions and fry for 8-10 minutes, or until they are browned.

12. As soon as the onions are caramelized, add a drop more oil, followed by the homemade Berbere spice, garlic, and ginger.

13. Stir fry for around 2-3 minutes, to allow the flavors to infuse, and the mixture is a rich brown. Do not allow to burn.

14. Next, add 2-3 cups of water. Add the chicken together with the tomato paste, basil and salt and continue cooking for 30 minutes.

15. Add the eggs and mix well to incorporate.

16. Continue cooking the chicken for 10 minutes, or until tender.

17. Adjust the consistency of the sauce using water or broth and salt as needed.

18. Serve with rice.

Recipe 37: Ireland - Spiced Beef Rib

Packed full of flavor and falling off the bone, spiced beef rib is a dish often seen on St Stephen's Day, celebrated on December 25th. Just make sure to prepare this dish well in advance.

Yield: 20-24

Preparation Time: 10mins

Cook Time: 6hours 30mins

Total Cook Time: 20hours 40mins*

Ingredient List:

- 1 medium turnip (chopped)
- 3 medium carrots (chopped)
- 1 yellow onion (sliced into rings)
- 6 pounds middle rib of beef (deboned, rolled)
- 1 fresh bay leaf
- Cold water
- 1 yellow onion (minced)

- ½ ounce curing salt
- 4 ounce brown sugar (moist)
- 6 teaspoons mixed spice
- 1 pound sea salt
- Pinches of black pepper, allspice, cloves, mixed herbs, mace, nutmeg, thyme
- Fresh parsley (finely chopped)

Instructions:

1. Take a large deep pan and lay the turnip, carrots and rings of onions in the base of the pan.

2. Set the beef on top and add the bay leaf. Pour over cold water to cover the beef.

3. Place the pan on the heat and boil for 6½ hours.

4. Take the pot off the heat and sandwich the beef between two plates, weigh down by placing a heavy object on the top plate. Set aside for 12-14 hours. Then remove the beef and tie with string.

5. In a bowl, combine the minced onion, curing salt, brown sugar, mixed spice, 1 pound of salt, black pepper, allspice, cloves, mixed herbs, mace, nutmeg, and thyme. Rub the mixture into the beef, massaging for 3-4 minutes.

6. Transfer the meat to a clay pot and cover with a lid.

7. Set aside in a cool, dry place, retuning to turn the meat once a day and massage with the spices.

8. When ready to serve, slice thinly!

*Plus 2 weeks standing time.

Recipe 38: France - Glazed Honey Roast Pork with Apples

This utterly delicious and moist honey roast pork with juicy apples would be a great dish to serve during le reveillon (or Christmas Eve meal) where families get together and feast long into the night.

Yield: 4

Preparation Time: 10mins

Cook Time: 1hour 30mins

Total Cook Time: 2hours 5mins

Ingredient List:
- 2½ pound pork loin roast
- Sea salt and black pepper
- 2 tablespoons organic honey

- 4 thyme sprigs
- 4 rosemary sprigs
- 6 tablespoons unsalted butter (chopped into cubes)
- 2 yellow onions (sliced into thin wedges)
- ½ cup dry apple cider
- 5 Gala apples (cored, sliced into quarters)

Instructions:

1. Preheat the main oven to 350 degrees F.

2. Set the pork in a roasting pan and season well with sea salt and black pepper. Drizzle with the organic honey.

3. Place the thyme and rosemary sprigs on top.

4. Scatter over the chopped butter and arrange the wedges of onion around the meat.

5. Place in the oven and roast for 45 minutes, remove and arrange the quartered apples around the pork in the roasting tin and return to the oven for another 45 minutes, a thermometer inserted into the thickest part of the pork should read 160 degrees F.

6. Remove the meat from the oven and set aside to rest 20-25 minutes.

7. Slice the pork thinly and serve with the apples and onions.

Recipe 39: India - Mutton Biryani

The Indian people love spicy dishes with complex flavors, and Christmas Day is no exception! Garnish with fried cashews, fresh coriander and onions and serve with an aromatic rice.

Yield: 4-6

Preparation Time: 15mins

Cook Time: 2hours 35mins

Total Cook Time: 2hours 50mins*

Ingredient List:

- 1 pound uncooked basmati rice
- 2 tablespoons grated coconut
- ¾ teaspoons chili powder
- ½ teaspoons dhaniya powder
- ¼ teaspoons turmeric
- ½ teaspoons garam masala
- 5 green chilis

- 2 tablespoons ginger paste
- 2 tablespoons garlic paste
- 1 pound mutton
- 1 cup water
- Pinch sea salt
- ½ cup oil
- 4 cinnamon sticks
- 4 cloves
- 4 cardamom pods
- 7 ounces yellow onion
- 10 whole cashews
- 3½ ounces tomato (chopped)
- 2 tablespoons curd
- 2 tablespoons ghee
- ½ bunch fresh mint (chopped)

Instructions:

8. Wash the rice and set aside to soak for 30 minutes.

9. Using a mortar and pestle, grind together the grated coconut, chili powder, dhaniya powder, turmeric, garam masala, green chilis, ginger, and garlic paste to a smooth paste.

10. Wash the mutton and add to a pressure cooker with the paste. Cook until ¾ done.

11. Pour in the water along with a pinch of salt.

12. In a heavy saucepan, heat the oil. Add the cinnamon, cloves, and cardamom, cook until fragrant and golden.

13. Add the onion and sauté until softened. Add the cashews and sauté for 30 seconds before adding the tomato and curd. Cook until the mixture is pulpy.

14. Add the cooked rice, heat and stir for 3-4 minutes.

15. Add the mutton to the saucepan.

16. Take 1½ cups of the cooking liquid from the pressure cooker and pour into the saucepan. Simmer for 12-15 minutes.

17. Pour over the ghee, cover with a lid and cook for 10-15 minutes.

18. Serve hot, with a fresh mint garnish.

Recipe 40: Greece - Veal Stew with Plums, Apricots, and Almonds

A hearty, filling stew packed with the rich flavor of dried fruits and cognac.

Yield: 4-6

Preparation Time: 15mins

Cook Time: 2hours 35mins

Total Cook Time: 2hours 50mins*

Ingredient List:

- 14-16 pieces of good quality stewing veal
- ⅔ cup olive oil
- 1⅓ pounds leeks (sliced)
- ⅓ cup cognac
- Fresh juice of 2 medium lemons
- 2 tablespoons soy sauce

- 2 medium carrots (sliced)
- 1 cup warm water
- Sea salt and black pepper
- 16 pitted dried apricots
- 12 pitted dried plums
- 16 whole almonds

Instructions:

1. Chop the veal into large chunks and wash well. Pat dry with kitchen paper.

2. Heat the olive oil in a saucepan, and add the veal.

3. Sauté the meat in batches until browned on all sides. Remove the veal using a slotted spoon and set aside on a plate, covered.

4. Sauté the leeks using the same oil until softened. Return the veal to the pan along with the cognac and lemon juice. Heat until the alcohol evaporates.

5. Add the soy sauce, carrots, water, sea salt and black pepper.

6. Cover with a lid, and on a low heat, simmer for 1½ hours.

7. After 1¼ hours, add the apricots, plums, and almonds. Stir and re-cover.

8. Serve hot!

Part 2

Popular Christmas and New Year Recipes

1) Traditional Honey Glazed Ham

This is perhaps the most traditional Christmas recipe that you can ever put together. The best part about this dish is that it makes plenty of ham to feed a large group of people and is great when paired with a side of mashed potatoes and healthy veggies.

Yield: 15 Servings

Cooking Time: 1 Hour and 35 Minutes

List of Ingredients:
- 1, 5 Pound Ham, Ready To Eat Variety
- ¼ Cup of Cloves, Whole
- ¼ Cup of Corn Syrup, Dark in Color
- 2 Cups of Honey, Raw
- 2/3 Cup of Butter, Soft and Melted

Procedure:

1. The first thing that you will want to do is preheat your oven to 325 degrees.

2. While your oven is heating up, score your ham and fill with your whole cloves. Then place your ham in a pan lined with aluminum foil.

3. Using a small sized saucepan, heat up your remaining ingredients until smooth in consistency. Remove from heat and keep warm.

4. Brush your ham with your freshly made glaze mixture generously.

5. Place your ham in your oven to bake for the next hour and 15 minutes. Make sure that you baste your ham every 10 to 15 minutes with your freshly made glaze.

6. During the last 5 minutes of baking, switch your oven to broil. Broil your ham until the glaze has been fully caramelized.

7. Then remove from your oven and allow your ham to cool slight before you serve it. Enjoy!

2) Bacon Wrapped Dates

If you have yet to find a way to make dates extremely tasty, then you have to try out this recipe for yourself. These little treats are incredibly delicious and make for the perfect finger food for any New Year's Eve party.

Yield: 32 Servings

Cooking Time: **1 Hour**

List of Ingredients:
- 1 Pound of Bacon, Sliced in Half
- 1 Pound of Dates, Fresh and Pitted
- 4 Ounces of Blue Cheese

Procedure:

1. The first thing that you will want to do is preheat your oven to 375 degrees.

2. While your oven is heating up slice your fresh dates in half. Then take a pinch or so of your blue cheese and place them into the center of your halved dates. Seal the dates together with each slice and wrap in place with a slice of your bacon.

3. Spear each wrapped date with a toothpick and arrange neatly on a generously greased baking dish.

4. Place into your oven to bake for the next 30 to 40 minutes or until your bacon is nice and crispy, making sure to turn over at least once during the baking process.

5. After this time remove from heat and arrange neatly on a serving platter. Serve immediately and enjoy!

3) Charleston Style Breakfast Casserole

If you are looking for the perfect breakfast recipe to cook up for a large group of people on New Year's Eve, this is the recipe for you. It is a great dish to prepare for breakfast or brunch and will easily please a large group.

Yield: 8 Servings

Cooking Time: 1 Hour and 20 Minutes

List of Ingredients:
- 12 Slices of Bacon, Freshly Cooked
- ¼ Cup of Butter, Soft and Melted
- 3 Cups of Croutons, Homemade Preferable
- 2 Cups of Cheddar Cheese, Finely Grated
- 6 Eggs, Large in Size and Beaten
- 1 ¾ Cups of Milk, Whole
- 1 Bell Pepper, Any Color and Finely Diced
- 1 tablespoon of Mustard, Prepared Ahead of Time

- Dash of Salt and Pepper for Taste

Procedure:

1. The first thing that you will want to do is place your bacon into a large sized skillet. Cover your bacon over medium to high heat and cook until brown in color. Once browned drain your bacon and crumble it finely. Set aside for later use.

2. Then preheat your oven to 325 degrees.

3. Next melt your butter. While your butter is melting grease a medium sized baking dish with a generous amount of cooking spray. Place your croutons into your baking dish and add in your melted butter. Sprinkle with a dash of your grated cheese and toss to evenly coat.

4. Then use a medium sized bowl and add in your remaining ingredients and whisk thoroughly to combine. Pour this mixture over your croutons. Top with your crumbled bacon.

5. Place your dish into your oven to bake for the next 40 minutes. After this time remove your dish from your bacon and allow to stand for at least 10 minutes before you serve it. Enjoy!

4) Tasty Pork and Sauerkraut

This is a traditional meal for New Year's Eve that I know you will love to enjoy. This makes for a great and filling meal that can pair excellently with any other dish you decide to whip up.

Yield: 12 Servings

Cooking Time: 6 Hours and 25 Minutes

List of Ingredients:
- 1 Pound of Pork Loin, Boneless and Roast Variety
- 2 Tablespoons of Olive Oil
- 2 Sprigs of Thyme Leaves, Fresh
- Dash of Salt and Pepper for Taste
- 4 Pounds of Sauerkraut
- 1 Pound of Kielbasa, Cut into Small Pieces

Procedure:

1. The first thing that you will want to do is preheat your broiler.

2. While your oven is preheating, place your pork roast into a roasting pan and brush with a generous amount of olive oil.

3. Season with your thyme leaves and salt and pepper for taste.

4. Then place your pork roast into your oven and broil for at least 10 minutes, making sure that your pork is lightly brown in various places.

5. While your pork is broiling, place half of your sauerkraut into a slow cooker and arrange your kielbasa around it.

6. After your pork is done roasting, place it into the center of your slow cooker. Cover your pork with your remaining sauerkraut.

7. Cover and cook on the highest setting for the next 6 hours. After this time serve and enjoy!

5) Chocolate Dipped Strawberries

This is perhaps the simplest chocolate covered strawberry recipe that you will ever find. Regardless of how simplistic it is, these strawberries are the tastiest you will ever find. I just know you are going to love them.

Yield: 24 Servings

Cooking Time: **15 Minutes**

List of Ingredients:
- 16 Ounces of Chocolate Chips, Milk Variety
- 2 Tablespoons of Shortening
- 1 Pound of Strawberries, Fresh and With Leaves

Procedure:

1. Using a double broiler, melt up your chocolate chips with your shortening, making sure to stir thoroughly until smooth in consistency.

2. Spear your fresh strawberries with toothpicks.

3. Then dip your strawberries in your chocolate mix.

4. Place your chocolate dipped strawberries on a baking sheet lined with parchment paper and set into your fridge to chill. Serve whenever you are ready.

6) Easy Roasted Veggies

This is a casserole dish that is packed full of filling vegetables that you will love to prepare again over and over again. Feel free to use fresh lemon juice instead of balsamic vinegar if you wish. Either this dish will leave a great taste in your mouth.

Yield: 12 Servings

Cooking Time: **55 Minutes**

List of Ingredients:
- 1 Butternut Squash, Small in Size and Cut into Cubes
- 2 Red Bell Peppers, Deseeded and Finely Diced
- 1 Sweet Potato, Peeled and Cut into Cubes
- 3 Yukon Potatoes, Gold in Color and Cut into Cubes
- 1 Red Onion, Cut Into Quarters
- 1 tablespoon of Thyme, Fresh and Finely Chopped
- 2 Tablespoons of Rosemary, Fresh and Finely Chopped

- ¼ Cup of Olive Oil
- 2 Tablespoons of Vinegar, Balsamic Variety
- Dash of Salt and Pepper for Taste

Procedure:

1. The first thing that you will want to do is preheat your oven to 475 degrees.

2. Then using a large sized bowl add in your first 4 ingredients. Follow up with your quartered red onions. Mix this mixture together until thoroughly mixed.

3. Using a small sized bowl, mix together your remaining ingredients together. Add to your chopped veggies and toss thoroughly to coat.

4. Spread your veggie mix in a large sized roasting pan and place into your preheated oven. Bake your veggies for the next 35 to 40 minutes, making sure to stir your mixture every 10 minutes or so. Cook until your veggies are browned in color and thoroughly cooked through.

7) Delicious Sweet Potato Casserole

This is a great dish to prepare if you have any picky eaters that you are looking to satisfy. This is a dish that is easy to make and sweet to taste.

Yield: 5 Servings

Cooking Time: **40 Minutes**

List of Ingredients:

- 2 Pounds of Sweet Potato, Peeled and Cut Into Cubes
- 2 Tablespoons of Orange Juice, Fresh
- ¾ Cup of Brown Sugar, Light and Packed
- 1/8 teaspoons of Nutmeg, Ground
- 2 Tablespoons of Butter, Soft and Cut into Cubes
- 1 Cup of Marshmallows, Miniature Variety

Procedure:

1. The first thing that you will want to do is preheat your oven to 350 degrees.

2. While your oven is heating up, use a large sized saucepan and cook up your sweet potatoes in some water seasoned with salt. Cook over medium heat for the next 20 minutes or until completely done and tender to the tough. Once tender drain your sweet potatoes and place back into your saucepan.

3. Next add in your remaining ingredients except for your miniature marshmallow and whip thoroughly using an electric mixture until smooth in consistency.

4. Pour your sweet potato mixture into a medium sized baking dish and top off with your miniature marshmallows.

5. Place into your oven to bake for the next 10 minutes or until your marshmallows are golden brown in color. Remove from oven and serve while still piping hot.

8) Hearty Black-Eyed Pea Gumbo

This is perhaps the most traditional winter time dinner that you can serve for either Christmas or New Years. It is an incredibly hearty dish that you can enjoy any time of the winter that you wish. This dish makes plenty, making it the perfect dish to cook up to feed a bunch of people.

Yield: 8 Servings

Cooking Time: 1 Hour and 10 Minutes

List of Ingredients:
- 1 tablespoon of Olive Oil
- 1 Onion, Medium in Size and Finely Chopped
- 1 Green Bell Pepper, Medium in Size and Finely Chopped
- 5 Celery Stalks, Finely Chopped

- 2 Cups of Chicken Broth
- 1 Cup of Rice, Brown in Color
- 4 Cans of Black Eyed Pease, With Liquid
- 1 Can of Tomatoes and Green Chiles, Finely Diced
- 2 Cloves of Garlic, Diced Finely
- 1 Can of Tomatoes, Diced Variety

Procedure:

1. Heat up a medium to large sized saucepan with your olive oil and set over medium heat. Once the oil is hot enough add in your next 3 ingredients and cook until they are completely tender.

2. Then pour in your remaining ingredients into your saucepan and stir until thoroughly combined.

3. Bring this mixture to a rolling boil. Reduce your heat to low and allow your dish to simmer for at least 45 minutes or until your brown rice is tender to the touch. If your soup is too thick, add in ¼ cup of water or more until it reaches your desired consistency.

4. Remove from heat and serve while still piping hot. Enjoy!

9) Healthy Kale and Yam Salad

If you are looking to enjoy something a little more on the healthy side this coming holiday season, then you cannot go wrong with this recipe. This salad has a subtle, yet sweet taste that you are going to want to enjoy every day.

Yield: 6 Servings

Cooking Time: 1 Hour and 15 Minutes

List of Ingredients:
- 2 Yams, Jewel Variety and Cut Into Small Cubes
- 2 Tablespoons of Olive Oil
- Dash of Salt and Pepper For Taste
- 1 tablespoon of Olive Oil
- 1 Onion, Large in Size and Sliced Finely
- 3 Cloves of Garlic, Minced
- 1 Bunch of Kale, Torn Roughly

- 2 Tablespoons of Vinegar, Red Wine Variety
- 1 teaspoon of Thyme, Fresh and Roughly Chopped

Procedure:

1. The first thing that you have to do is preheat your oven to 400 degrees.

2. While your oven is heating up toss your yams with your olive oil in a medium to large sized bowl, making sure to toss until thoroughly coated. Season with a dash of salt and pepper and toss again. Arrange your yams on a large sized baking sheet that is generously greased.

3. Place your yams into your oven and bake until your yams are tender. This should take at least 20 to 25 minutes. After this time remove from your oven and cool. Once it reaches room temperature place your yams into your fridge to chill.

4. While your yams are chilling, heat up you remaining olive oil in a large sized skillet and set over medium to high heat. Add in your onions and garlic and sauté until it reaches a golden brown color. This should take at least 15 minutes.

5. After this time add in your kale and cook until the kale wilts. Remove from heat.

6. Add this mixture into a medium sized bowl and all to cool down to room temperature. Once thoroughly cooled place into your fridge to chill.

7. Once all of your ingredients are chilled, combine your kale mix, yam mix and remaining ingredients together in a large sized salad bowl, making sure to toss thoroughly to evenly combine. Serve immediately and enjoy.

10) Christmas Style Pear Salad

If you are looking to enjoy something a little more light for this holiday season, then you cannot go wrong with this awesome salad recipe. It is light and healthy, making it the perfect recipe to enjoy without having to feel guilty.

Yield: 6 Servings

Cooking Time: **30 Minutes**

Ingredients for Your Salad:
- 1 Head of Lettuce, Torn Roughly Into Small Pieces
- 3 Pears, Peeled, Cored and Finely Chopped
- 5 Ounces of Cheese, Roquefort Variety and Crumbled
- 1 Avocado, Peeled, Pitted and Finely Diced
- ½ Cup of Onions, Green in Color and Sliced Thinly
- ¼ Cup of Sugar, White
- ½ Cup of Pecans, Crushed

Ingredients for Your Dressing:
- 1/3 Cup of Olive Oil
- 3 Tablespoons of Vinegar, Red Wine Variety
- 1 ½ teaspoons of Sugar, White
- 1 ½ teaspoons of Mustard, Prepared Ahead of Time
- 1 Clove of Garlic, Finely Chopped
- ½ teaspoons of Salt
- Dash of Black Pepper for Taste

Procedure:

1. Use a medium to large sized skillet and place it over medium heat. Add in your pecans and sugar together and stir vigorously until your sugar has fully melted and the pecans are caramelized. Remove from heat and transfer to some waxed paper to cool.

2. Once your pecans are fully cooled, break the nuts into small pieces.

3. Next make your dressing. To do this mix together all of your ingredients for all of your dressing ingredients in a small sized bowl. Whisk vigorously until thoroughly combined.

4. Next take a large sized serving bowl and place neat layers of your remaining salad ingredients. Pour your freshly made dressing over your dressing and add in your pecans. Toss to thoroughly mix and serve immediately. Enjoy!

11) Homemade Tamales

While this is a traditional Mexican recipe, this is still a dish that can be made for Christmas or New Years. This makes for a truly delicious dish that you will want to make over and over again.

Yield: 16 Servings

Cooking Time: 3 Hours and 35 Minutes

Ingredients for Your Tamale Filling:
- 1 ¼ Pounds of Pork Loin
- 1 Onion, Large in Size and Cut Into Halves
- 1 Clove of Garlic, Minced
- 4 Chile Pods, California Style
- 2 Cups of Water
- 1 ½ teaspoons of Salt

Ingredients for Your Tamale Dough:

- 2 Cups of Masa Harina
- 1 Can of Beef Broth
- 1 teaspoon of Baking Powder
- ½ teaspoons of Salt
- 2/3 Cup of Lard
- 1 Pack of Corn Husks, Dried
- 1 Cup of Sour Cream

Procedure:

1. The first thing that you will want to do is place your pork into a large Dutch oven. Add your onions and minced garlic, along with a generous amount of water to cover your pork.

2. Allow your pork mix to come to a rolling boil and then reduce the heat to a simmer. Continue cooking until your pork has fully cooked through. This should take about 2 hours.

3. Next prepare your chile pods. To do this use rubber gloves and remove the seeds and stems from the chilies. Then place into a medium to large sized saucepan with at least 2 cups of water. Allow to simmer of low heat for the next 20 minutes. After this time remove from heat and set aside to cool.

4. Once cooled pour your chilies and water into a blender and puree on the highest setting until smooth in consistency. Once smooth strain this mixture through a fine mesh strainer. Add in your salt and stir to combine. Set aside.

5. Next shred your cooked pork and set into a bowl with at least 1 cup of your Chile sauce mix.

6. You will then have to place your corn husks in a large sized bowl filled with warm water.

7. Then use a separate large sized bowl and beat together your lard with your broth using an electric mixer until fluffy in texture. Add in your Masa harina, dash of salt and baker's style baking powder. Stir to thoroughly combine, making sure to add more broth if needed until your mixture begins to form a soft dough.

8. Next spread your tamale dough over your corn husks. Then place at least one tablespoon of your meat filling directly in the center. Roll your tamales and place them into a steamer to steam for at least 1 hour.

9. After this time remove your tamales from the corn husks and drizzle with your leftover Chile sauce mix. Top off with some sour cream and serve right away.

12) Delicious Eggnog

If you are a huge fan of Eggnog, I know for a fact that you are going to love this recipe. This recipes has been perfected over the years, resulting in an Eggnog recipe that you are going to want to make over and over again.

Yield: 12 Servings

Cooking Time: 6 Hours and 28 Minutes

List of Ingredients:
- 4 Cups of Milk, Whole
- 5 Cloves, Whole
- ½ teaspoons of Vanilla, Pure
- 1 teaspoon of Cinnamon, Ground
- 12 Eggs, Yolks Only
- 1 ½ Cups of Sugar, White
- 2 ½ Cups of Rum, Light and Your Favorite Kind

- 4 Cups of Cream, Light Variety
- 2 teaspoons of Vanilla, Pure
- ½ teaspoons of Nutmeg, Ground

Procedure:

1. Using a medium to large sized saucepan and combine your first 3 ingredients together. Set over low heat and cook for at least 5 minutes. Let this mixture come to a boil. Once boiling, remove from heat and set aside.

2. In a large sized bowl add in your egg yolks and sugar and whisk thoroughly until combined and fluffy in consistency.

3. Add your hot mixture to your egg yolk mixture. Pour into your saucepan and continue heating until thick in consistency. Remember, do not let this mixture come to a boil. Remove and strain through a fine mesh strainer and allow to cool for at least an hour.

4. Stir in your remaining ingredients to your mixture and stir to evenly incorporate. Place into a bowl, cover and place into your fridge to chill overnight. Enjoy whenever you are ready.

13) Cheese and Ham Party Sandwiches

These tiny little sandwiches are practically perfect for any little party that you may be throwing. I guarantee that your guests will love these snacks, they will be begging you for the recipe.

Yield: 24 Servings

Cooking Time: **35 Minutes**

List of Ingredients:
- ¾ Cup of Butter, Melted
- 1 ½ Tablespoons of Dijon Mustard, Your Favorite Kind
- 1 ½ teaspoons of Worcestershire Sauce
- 1 ½ Tablespoons of Poppy Seeds
- 1 tablespoon of Onion, Dried and Minced
- 24 Sandwich Rolls, Mini
- 1 Pound of Deli Ham, Thinly Sliced

- 1 Pound of Swiss Cheese, Thinly Sliced

Procedure:

1. First preheat your oven to 350 degrees. While your oven is heating up lightly grease a medium to large sized baking dish with a generous amount of cooking spray.

2. Then use a medium sized bowl and mix together your first 5 ingredients until evenly mixed.

3. Then take the rolls and cut off the tops. Place your bottom roll pieces onto your baking dish.

4. Next neatly layer your ham and cheese on your rolls and cover with your tops.

5. Pour your butter mixture over the top of the rolls and place into the oven to bake.

6. Bake your rolls in your oven until they are lightly brown in color and your cheese has fully melted. This should take about 20 minutes.

7. After this time remove from oven and slice into halves. Serve immediately and enjoy!

14) Decadent Banana Bread

Why tarnish the delicious taste of banana when you make this type of bread? With this recipe you can make the most moist and delicious banana bread that is packed with that sweet banana flavor that we all know and love.

Yield: 12 Servings

Cooking Time: 1 Hour and 20 Minutes

List of Ingredients:
- 2 Cups of Flour, All Purpose Variety
- 1 teaspoon of Baker's Style Baking Soda
- ¼ teaspoons of Salt
- ½ Cup of Butter, Soft
- ¾ Cup of Brown Sugar, Light and Packed
- 2 Eggs, Large in Size and Beaten
- 2 1/3 Cups of Bananas, Ripe and Mashed

Procedure:

1. The first thing that you will want to do is preheat your oven to 350 degrees. While your oven is heating up grease a medium to large sized loaf pan with a generous amount of cooking spray.

2. Then use a large sized bowl and combine all of your ingredients together until well blended and your bread batter is slightly moist.

3. Pour your batter into your greased loaf pan and place into your oven.

4. Let your bread bake for the next 60 to 65 minutes or until your bread is fully cooked through.

5. After this time remove your oven and allow your bread to cool in the pan for at least 10 minutes. Then remove it from your pan and place onto a wire rack to fully cool. Serve whenever you are ready.

15) Appetizer Cocktail Meatballs

This is one appetizer dish that you are going to make a whole lot of. I guarantee that once your guests get a taste of these tasty treats, these will quickly disappear.

Yield: 10 Servings

Cooking Time: 1 Hour and 45 Minutes

List of Ingredients:
- 1 Pound of Ground Beef, Lean
- 1 Egg, Large in Size and Beaten
- 2 Tablespoons of Water
- ½ Cup of Bread Crumbs
- 3 Tablespoons of Onion, Minced
- 1 Can of Cranberry Sauce, Jellied Variety
- ¾ Cup of Chili Sauce
- 1 tablespoon of Brown Sugar, Light and Packed

- 1 ½ teaspoons of Lemon Juice, Fresh

Procedure:

1. The first thing that you will want to do is preheat your oven to 350 degrees.

2. While your oven is heating up use a large sized bowl and mix together your first 5 ingredients until thoroughly mixed. Roll this mixture into small sized meatballs.

3. Place your meatballs onto a generously greased baking sheet and place into your oven to bake for at least 20 to 25 minutes, making sure to turn at least once during the baking process.

4. Then use a small sized saucepan and place it over low heat. Mix your remaining ingredients together until thoroughly mixed.

5. Once your meatballs are fully cooked, dip them in your sauce and spear with toothpicks. Serve immediately and enjoy!

16) Easy Spinach Dip

This is a great dish to make as a great tasting appetizer. You can prepare this dish and serve it alongside a side of chips or even bread. Either way I know you are going to love it.

Yield: 6 Servings

Cooking Time: 6 Hours and 15 Minutes

List of Ingredients:
- 1 Cup of Mayonnaise, Your Favorite Kind
- 1, 16 Ounce Container of Sour Cream
- 1 Pack of Leek Soup Mix, Dry
- 1 Can of Chestnuts, Water Variety, Drained and Finely Chopped
- ½ Pack of Spinach, Frozen, Thawed, Drained and Finely Chopped
- 1 Pound Loaf of Sourdough

Procedure:

1. Use a medium sized bowl mix together all of your ingredients except for your sourdough bread. Mix until evenly blended.

2. Cover and place into your fridge to chill for at least 6 hours or overnight preferable.

3. While your dip is chilling remove the top of your sourdough bread.

4. Pour your chilled dip into your bread and serve right away. Enjoy!

17) Tasty Prime Rib

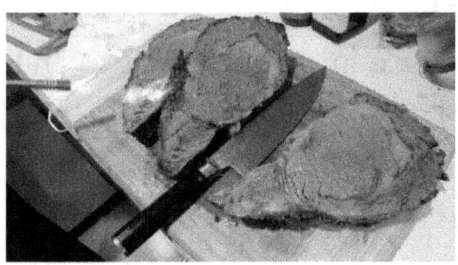

If you are unsure of what kind of dinner entrée to serve this upcoming Christmas day, you need to try your hand at making this traditional Christmas dish. This makes the moistest and succulent prime rib you have ever tasted!

Yield: 15 Servings

Cooking Time: 1 Hour and 40 Minutes

List of Ingredients:
- 1 Pound of Prime Rib
- 10 Cloves of Garlic, Minced
- 2 Tablespoons of Olive Oil, Extra Virgin Variety
- 2 teaspoons of Salt
- 2 teaspoons of Black Pepper
- 2 teaspoons of Thyme, Dried

Procedure:

1. The first thing that you will want to do is place your prime rib into a large sized roasting pan with the fat side facing up.

2. Then use a small sized bowl and mix together your remaining ingredients, stirring well to evenly combine.

3. Spread your olive oil mixture over the top of your roast and let your roast sit in the juice for at least a couple of minutes to 1 hour.

4. While your roast is sitting out preheat your oven to 500 degrees.

5. Place your roast into your oven and bake for the next 20 minutes. Then reduce the heat of your oven to 325 degree.

6. Continue to cook your roast for an additional 60 to 75 minutes or until the internal temperature reaches 135 degrees.

7. After this time remove your roast and let it sit out for at least 10 to 15 minutes before you carve it.

18) Easy Baked Kale Chips

This is a tasty and healthy snack recipe that you will want to make over and over again. Just like potato chips, I know after you have one you will be wanting more. This is a great dish to serve for any occasion and it is one that your guests will be begging for the recipe.

Yield: 6 Servings

Cooking Time: **10 Minutes**
List of Ingredients:
- 1 Bunch of Kale, Fresh
- 1 tablespoon of Olive Oil
- 1 teaspoon of Salt

Procedure:

1. The first thing that you will want to do is preheat your oven to 350 degrees. While your oven is heating up, line a cookie sheet with some parchment paper.

2. Now take a sharp knife and remove the stems for your kale. Then chop your kale into small sized pieces.

3. Wash your freshly chopped kale with some water and place into a bowl. Drizzle your olive oil and dash of salt over your kale and toss to thoroughly combined.

4. Place onto your parchment lined baking sheet and place into your oven to bake. Bake for the next 10 to 15 minutes or until the edges are browned. Remove from oven and serve right away. Enjoy!

19) Decadent Chocolate Trifle

Here is yet another great tasting and decadent dessert recipe that you are going to want to make over and over again. I guarantee that once your guests get a bite of this treat, they will be lining up for more to enjoy.

Yield: 12 Servings

Cooking Time: 8 Hours and 55 Minutes

List of Ingredients:
- 1 Pack of Brownie Mix, Your Favorite Kind
- 1 Pack of Pudding Mix, Instant Variety
- ½ Cup of Water
- 1 Can of Milk, Condensed and Sweetened
- 1, 8 Ounce Container of Whipped Topping, Frozen and Thawed

- 1, 12 Ounce Container of Whipped Topping, Frozen and Thawed
- 1 Car of Chocolate, Milk Variety and Your Favorite Kind

Procedure:

1. The first thing that you will want to do is prepare your brownie mix however the package directs you to do so. Once baked, allow your brownies to cool and then cut into small squares.

2. Then use a large sized bowl and combine your next 3 ingredients together until smooth in consistency. Fold in your first whipped topping container and continue to mix until thoroughly combined.

3. Next take out a few trifle glasses or small ice cream dish and place half of your brownies, followed by half of your pudding mix and your whipped topping. Continue to repeat your layers until all of your ingredients have been used up.

4. Garnish your dishes with some shaved chocolate and place into your fridge to chill for the next 8 hours or so. After this time serve right away and enjoy!

20) Apple Caramel Pork Chops

You will not be able to eat any other kind of pork chop recipe once you have tried this dish out for yourself. This dish makes for the perfect Christmas or New Year's Eve dinner dish. For the tastiest results I highly recommend that you serve this main course with a side of mashed potatoes or green beans.

Yield: 4 Servings

Cooking Time: **45 Minutes**

List of Ingredients:
- 4 Pork Chops, Thick Cut
- 1 teaspoon of Vegetable Oil
- 2 Tablespoons of Brown Sugar, Light and Packed
- Dash of Salt and Pepper For Taste
- 1/8 teaspoons of Cinnamon, Ground

- 1/8 teaspoons of Nutmeg, Ground
- 2 Tablespoons of Butter, Unsalted
- 2 Apples, Tart Variety, Peeled, Cored and Finely Sliced
- 3 Tablespoons of Pecans, Crushed and Optional

Procedure:

1. The first thing that you will want to do is preheat your oven to 175 degrees. While your oven is heating up place a medium to large sized baking dish inside of the oven to warm up.

2. Then use a large sized skillet over medium to high heat. While your skillet is heating up brush your pork chops generously with some oil and place into your pan. Cook your pork chops for at least 5 to 6 minutes or until they are fully cooked. Transfer these pork chops to your warm baking dish and place into your oven to keep warm.

3. Use a small sized bowl and thoroughly combine your remaining ingredients including your pecans if you are using them and stir to thoroughly combine. Pour this mixture into another skillet and cook over medium to high heat until your apples are tender to the touch.

4. Remove your apples from this mixture and place on top of your pork chops.

5. Continue cooking your sauce until it is thick in consistency and spoon over your warmed pork chops. Serve immediately and enjoy!

21) Cheesy Baked Tortellini

This is such an easy recipe for you to make, you won't be able to get enough of it. To give this recipe a touch of Italian taste, add some Italian sausage to it to make for a classic yet delicious New Year's dish that you will want to make every year.

Yield: 6 Servings

Cooking Time: **30 Minutes**

List of Ingredients:

- 2 Packs of Tortellini, Filled with Cheese
- 1 Jar of Marinara Sauce, Your Favorite Kind
- 1 Jar of Alfredo Sauce, your Favorite Kind
- 1 Box of Spinach, Frozen, Thawed and Finely Chopped
- 1 tablespoon of Italian Seasoning, Dried

- 1 Pack of Mozzarella Cheese, Finely Shredded
- ¼ Cup of Parmesan Cheese, Fresh and Finely Grated
- 1 teaspoon of Italian Seasoning, Dried

Procedure:

1. Take out a large sized pot and fill it with enough water to cover your pasta. Season the water with salt and bring to a rolling boil. Once boiling add in your pasta and cook until the pasta is tender to the touch. Once tender drain your pasta.

2. Next preheat your oven to broil. While your oven is heating up generously grease a medium sized baking dish with some butter.

3. Then bring together your next 4 ingredients into a medium sized saucepan and heat over low to medium heat. Let your mixture cook for the next 10 minutes at a simmer.

4. After this time add your cooked pasta to your sauce and stir thoroughly to combine. Remove from heat.

5. Pour your pasta mix into your greased baking dish and top with your remaining ingredients.

6. Place into your oven to broil for a minute or so or until your cheese has browned and fully melted. Remove from oven and allow to cool slightly before serving.

22) Filling Cheese and Broccoli Soup

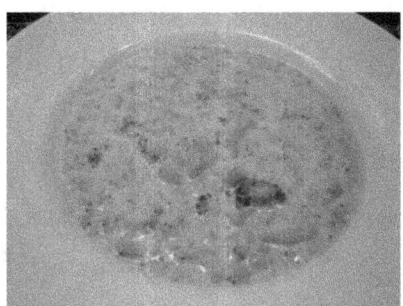

If you are looking to prepare a light and tasty dinner or lunch entrée, this is the perfect recipe for you. This is a flavorful soup that can be made for nearly any kind of occasion.

Yield: 12 Servings

Cooking Time: **40 Minutes**

List of Ingredients:

- ½ Cup of Butter, Soft and Melted
- 1 Onion, Medium in Size and Finely Chopped
- 1 Pack of Broccoli, Frozen and Finely Chopped
- 4 Cans of Chicken Broth
- 1 Pound of Cheese, Loaf Variety and Cut Into Cubes
- 2 Cups of Milk, Whole
- 1 tablespoon of Garlic, Powder

- 2/3 Cup of Cornstarch
- 1 Cup of Water

Procedure:

1. Use a large sized stockpot and melt your butter by placing the stockpot over medium to high heat. Once your butter has melted add in your onions and cook until soft and translucent.

2. Add in your broccoli and chicken broth. Reduce the heat and allow your mixture to simmer for at least 10 to 15 minutes.

3. Add in your cheese cubes and continue cooking until the cheese has fully melted. Once melted add in your milk and garlic powder. Stir to thoroughly combine.

4. Then take out a small sized bowl and add in your water and cornstarch. Stir vigorously until your cornstarch fully dissolves. Stir this mixture into your soup and continue to stir until your soup is thick in consistency.

5. Remove from stove top and serve while your soup is still piping hot. Enjoy!

23) Easy Squash Risotto

This is a great tasting recipe to bring in the holiday season. Butternut squash is full of sweet flavor and creamy in consistency, making it a great dish to enjoy as a full meal or as a tasty side dish.

Yield: 4 Servings

Cooking Time: **55 Minutes**

List of Ingredients:
- 2 Cups of Butternut Squash, Cut Into Small Cubes
- 2 Tablespoons of Butter, Soft and Melted
- ½ an Onion, Minced
- 1 Cup of Rice, Arborio Variety
- 1/3 Cup of Wine, Dry and White
- 5 Cups of Chicken Stock, Homemade Preferable and Hot
- ¼ Cup of Parmesan Cheese, Finely Grated

- Dash of Salt and Pepper For Taste

Procedure:

1. The first thing that you will want to do is place your squash into a steamer and place in a saucepan. Add in your water to your pan and allow it to come to a boil over medium to high heat. Allow your squash to steam cook until the squash is tender. This should take about 10 to 15 minutes.

2. After this time remove your squash and mash thoroughly with a fork until fluffy in consistency.

3. Next melt your butter in a large sized saucepan over medium to high heat. Once heated add in your onions and sauté them for at least 2 minutes or until your onions are soft. Once soft add in your rice and continue cooking for at least 5 minutes or until your rice is glossy in butter and your onions brown on the edges.

4. Then add in your white wine and continue to cook, making sure that you stir vigorously until it has fully evaporated.

5. Add in your mashed squash and half of your chicken stock, making sure to continue stirring. Add in your remaining chicken stock and stir to thoroughly combine. Continue to stir your mixture until your risotto until it is creamy in consistency.

6. Last add your dash of salt and pepper and grated Parmesan cheese and stir to blend in. Remove from heat and serve while still piping hot.

24) Tasty and Decadent Carrot Cake

This recipe makes for the tastiest dessert dish that you will have the pleasure of enjoying. Keep in mind that this recipe calls for the use of pecans, which you can leave out if you don't want to use them. Either way I know you are going to love this cake!

Yield: 18 Servings

Cooking Time: **2 Hours**

Ingredients For Your Cake:
- 4 Eggs, Large in Size and Beaten
- 1 ¼ Cups of Vegetable Oil
- 2 Cups of Sugar, White
- 2 teaspoons of Vanilla, Pure
- 2 Cups of Flour, All Purpose Variety
- 2 teaspoons of Baker's Style Baking Powder

- ½ teaspoons of Salt
- 2 teaspoons of Cinnamon, Ground
- 3 Cups of Carrots, Finely Grated
- 1 Cup of Pecans, Finely Chopped

Ingredients For Your Frosting:
- ½ Cup of Butter, Soft and Melted
- 8 Ounces of Cream Cheese, Soft
- 4 Cups of Confectioner's Sugar
- 1 teaspoon of Vanilla, Pure
- 1 Cup of Pecans, Finely Chopped

Procedure:

1. The first thing that you will want to do is preheat your oven to 350 degrees. While your oven is heating up light grease and flour a medium to large sized baking pan.

2. Use a large sized bowl and beat together your first 4 ingredients until thoroughly combined. Then mix in your next 6 ingredients until evenly mixed.

3. Gently fold in your chopped pecans until thoroughly combined.

4. Pour your freshly made batter into your greased and floured pan and place into your oven.

5. Bake your mixture in your oven for the next 40 to 50 minutes or until your cake is fully baked through. Remove from oven and let your cake cool in the pan for

the next 10 minutes before transferring to a cooling rack to cool completely.

6. While your cake is cooling, prepare your frosting next. To do this combine all of your frosting ingredients together in a small sized bowl. Then use an electric mixer and beat your frosting until smooth and creamy in consistency.

7. Once your cake has fully cooled, spread your frosting across the top of it and serve whenever you are ready.

25) Classic Artichoke Bruschetta

If you are a fan of classic artichoke dip, then I know for certain that you are going to love this recipe. This dish is based off its dip predecessor and is always a huge hit among crowds. I know for certain that your friends and family are going to love this dish.

Yield: 8 Servings

Cooking Time: **20 Minutes**

List of Ingredients:

- 1, 6.5 Ounce Jar of Artichoke, Hearts Only, Drain and Finely Chopped
- ½ Cup of Romano Cheese, Finely Grated
- 1/3 Cup of Red Onion, Finely Chopped
- 5 Tablespoons of Mayonnaise
- 1 Baguette, French Style and Cut Into Thick Slices

Procedure:

1. The first thing that you will want to do is preheat your broiler.

2. Then take a medium sized bowl and mix all of your ingredients together except for your baguette slices. Stir thoroughly to combine.

3. Top your thick baguette slices with your artichoke mixture and place onto a baking pan lined with some aluminum foil.

4. Place your pan into your oven and broil your bread for the next 2 minutes or until your artichoke topping is bubbly and light brown in color. Serve immediately and enjoy!

26) Creamy Lentil Soup

This soup recipe originally originated in Hungary where it is considered to be one of the most traditional dishes that you can enjoy. Making this dish is a great way to bring in the New Year in a filling and tasty way.

Yield: 8 Servings

Cooking Time: 1 Hour and 30 Minutes

List of Ingredients:
- 2 Tablespoons of Olive Oil
- 2 Onions, Large in Size and Cut Into Small Cubes
- 1 teaspoon of Garlic, Minced
- 3 Carrots, Fresh, Large in Size and Finely Diced
- 2 Stalks of Celery, Finely Diced
- 3 ½ Cups of Tomatoes, Crushed
- 1 ½ Cups of Lentils, Soaked and Drained

- ½ teaspoons of Salt
- ½ teaspoons of Black Pepper, Ground
- ¾ Cup of Wine, White
- 2 Bay Leaves, Fresh
- 7 Cups of Chicken Stock, Homemade Preferable
- 1 Sprig of Parsley, Finely Chopped and Fresh
- ½ teaspoons of Paprika
- ½ Cup of Parmesan Cheese, Finely Grated

Procedure:

1. Using a large sized stockpot, add in your onions and olive oil and cook until your onions are glossy in color.

2. Then stir in your minced garlic, paprika, finely diced carrots and stalks of celery. Sauté for the next 10 minutes or until your veggies are nice and tender.

3. Once your veggies are tender, add in your remaining ingredients except for your parsley and Parmesan cheese and stir to thoroughly combine.

4. Let this mixture cook until it comes to a rolling boil. Once boiling reduce the heat to a simmer and allow your soup to cook for at least 1 hour or until your lentils are tender.

5. Remove from heat and serve in soup bowl. Garnish with some Parmesan cheese and parsley and serve while still piping hot.

www.ingramcontent.com/pod-product-compliance
Lightning Source LLC
Chambersburg PA
CBHW072020070526
44583CB00015B/1560